Basic Software Concepts

Containership – Equilibrium

Peter Oye Sagay

ISBN-13: 978-0692518298 (TECTechnics)

ISBN-10: 0692518290

Dedication

To my dearest wife Kimmy. The woman behind the man
To my dearest daughter Seyi. My princess.
My world is beautiful because they are in it.

Acknowledgment

The vastness of the Knowledge – Information Continuum is the direct result of the contributions of many men, women and children who over the centuries, and in their respective ways have shared their knowledge with humanity. We are all intellectually, spiritually and bodily enriched because they shared their knowledge. So to these great individuals I say thank you!

I was born the seventh child of my mother and the twenty-first child of my father. Both were honorable and successful parents from whom I received true and great love. My childhood memories of my father are lovely and joyous. He was a very loving father. We had a great time: we played, laughed and talked whenever we were together.

All through her life my mother was always a loving mother. She raised me and took care of me from birth to adulthood. I lacked nothing I needed. Whatever positiveness has come out of my life, it is primarily due to her.

My elementary and secondary school years were fun years. I was an excellent student with minimal effort. However, my mother and my uncle were the individuals who made sure I had an excellent academic foundation. I had no plans for that. My plans were centered around being a playboy and I played well. The solid academic foundation became very useful in later years when my focused changed to being an intellectual. Additionally, my lovely wife *Kimmy* is truly a blessing . So to my mother, *Princess Margaret Seyigbemi Simate*, *my father. Chief William. A Sagay*, my uncle *Hon. Andrew A. E. Sagay* and my wife *Kimberlee*, I say thank you!

Content

Introduction

Computers and the software that run them are everywhere. They solve various types of problems very impressively. No matter how complex these problems are, the software that solve these problems with the aid of the computers are in essence made up of simple foundational concepts. The objective of this book is to enunciate these concepts in a format that is consistent with the *conceptual infra-structure* of the Knowlege-Information Continuum.

This *conceptual infra-structure* was established by Nature. It is entirely made up of the following 7 universal concepts: *containership*, *identity*, *force*, *motion*, *change*, *grouping/interaction* and *equilibrium*. I call this Nature's template, *TECTechnics,* a word derived from the *Theory of Existential Continuums.* Information about this theory is at **www.tectechnics.com**.

Consequently, the contents of Basis Software Concepts are presented according to the following format:
Chapter one, *software containership*, is about the *residence* and *workspace* of *software*.
Chapter two, *software identity*, uniquely defines *software* and describes how it is created.
Chapter three, s*oftware force*, describes the *nature* of *software force*.
Chapter four, *software motion,* describes the *motions of software* in its *workspace*.
Chapter five, *software change,* describes why and how software change.
Chapter six, s*oftware groupings/interactions,* describes the primary software groups and software interactions.
Chapter seven, software equilibrium, describes *software equilibrium*.

The 7 Basic Software Concepts

Containership

Identity

Force

Motion

Change

Group/Interaction

Equilibrium

1 Software Containership

1.0 What is Containership?

In this presentation, *space* means the *inside* of any partition of the *Universe*. In other words, an occupiable sub-space of the Universe. *Space* is a *container,* that is, it is able to hold matter. This ability of *space* is its *containership property*. The *containership property* of space allows matter to reside in space and it is in the context of this residency that events occur in space.

Software Containership refers to the spaces it occupies. These spaces are its *static space* and its *dynamic space*.

1.1 Static Space

The *static space* of software is its *residence*. It is where it lives until it is called to duty. In this static space there is no resultant force acting on the software, so it is at rest and a *force-in-waiting* (a doer waiting to be called to action). In general, software resides in secondary storage media. Examples are magnetic storage media such as the hard disks and thumb disks; and optical storage media such as the DVDs and CDs.

1.2 Dynamic Space

The *dynamic space* of software is its *workspace*. It is in this space that it is a doer. *Software* works incessantly in this dynamic space until it is interupted or terminated.

The dynamic space of software is an electronic space that consists of numerous integrated electronic circuits. We shall examine some of the basic concepts of these circuits in chapter three.

1.3 Chapter summary

Software containership refers to the spaces software occupies. These spaces can broadly be categorized into two spaces: its static space (residence) and its dynamic space (workspace).

In its static space (mostly in secondary storage media), *software* is a *force-in-waiting* until it is called to action. In its dynamic space (mostly an electronic environment) *software* is incessantly at work until it is interupted or terminated.

2 Software Identity

2.0 What is Identity

Identity refers to the unique characteristic(s) of an entity. The characteristic(s) must be recognizable when presented. For example, consider a new-born baby. At birth, some characteristics are instantly associated with the baby: the gender of the baby, the parents of the baby, the time and place of birth. These characteristics are helpful components of the baby's identity but they are not sufficient for an objective identification of the baby. For instance, there are other babies of the same gender and the parents may have other babies.

The parentage of the baby may be a unique characteristic if the baby is the only child of the parents and the parents have unique identity. But this characteristic will be difficult to manage in the context of a large population. Also, there may be other babies with the same time and place of birth.
So, the parents assign a name to the baby, say *Ariya Simasa* in order to increase the number of components that constitute the baby's identity.

For Ariya's family, friends and most of the people she will encounter during her life, her name in addition to the other components of her individuality are sufficient to identify her even though the components are all still subjective. So, the Government comes in to make her identity objective and assigns a unique *social number* to *Ariya Simasa* which in addition to the other circumstances of her birth establishes her unique *Identity.*

In general, an entity's *identity* must be unique, objectively verifiable and generally acceptable in the context of the existential states of the entity.

2.1 Definition of Software

The word *software* does not reveal its meaning as it is used in computer science. It is a compound word that consists of *soft* and *ware*. The word *ware* has some contextual significance in the sense that its meanings as an *article of commerce* and as a *set of something* (e.g. silverware, tableware) are applicable to *software*. *Software* is usually an article of commerce and as we shall see when it is defined, it is also a set of *something*. Humans often create words that do not directly reveal their meanings. So, they define the words in order to establish their meanings. The following is a simple definition of software:

Software is the set of instructions a machine (usually the computer) must execute in order to arrive at the solution of a problem.

The uniqueness in the definition of software is that the instructions that constitute it must be machine executable.

The earliest usage of the word soft-ware (note the hyphenation) was in 1850 AD. In that time, soft-ware (note the hyphenation) was used in the context of garbage and it referred to matter that would decompose while hard-ware referred to any matter that does not decompose.

The word software as is now used in computer science, first occurred in the January 9-10, 1956 Proceedings of the *Second National Symposium on Quality Control* and Reliability on Electronics in Washington D.C. However, statistician John W. Tukey (1915 AD-2000 AD) is generally regarded as the person who coined the word software because he is the earliest documented user of the word software.

He used the word software in his article The *Teaching of Concrete Mathematics* in the January 1958 issue of American Mathematical Monthly. The following is the passage that referred to software: "*Today the "software" comprising the carefully planned interpretive routines, compilers, and other aspects of automative programming are at least as important to the modern electronic calculator as its "hardware" of tubes, transistors, wires, tapes and the like"*.

The word *software* became popular at about the late 1970s when manufacturers of the personal computers craftily marketed the personal computers and the application programs that came with them as indispensable necessities. Personal computer marketers and educators saw the "comparative beauty" in the double-word, hardware-software, so they based their marketing and educational campaigns accordingly. These marketing campaigns were so successful that the word *software*, became a popular and preferable synonym for codes and computer programs.

2.2 Software Creation

The creation of software begins in the human mind in the form of a problem. Once the problem is thoroughly understood and defined, the programmer creates an ***algorithm*** (instructions that lead to the solution of the problem) for the problem. Next a source code is created by writing the algorithm in a preferred programming language.

2.2.1 Methods and Data

The source code contains all the steps required to solve the problem of interest. Methods (also called functions) are the building blocks used to construct the source code. A method is the series of acts (instructions) required to realize a desired result. In computer programming, the acts are the instructions submitted to the processor and the desired results are the processor's output on execution of the instructions. These instructions often act-upon data. So methods and data are usually co-dependent in a source code. In fact, a source code is essentially mostly about methods and the data they act-upon. For example, consider the following method:

Put the book on the table in your bag -----(1)

It is clear that (1) is an instruction that entails two acts: the taking of the book from the table and the putting of the book in the bag. It is also clear that the book is the object acted-upon. What is not so clear in instruction (1) is the spaces implied in it: the trip to the table and to the bag and the spaces occupied by the book and the bag. These concepts are basic and are present in all source codes. In fact, most of what a software does is moving stuff (specifically bytes) around inside the computer.

2.2.2 Program Flow

Program flow refers to the order in which instructions are executed. Normally, the instructions within a method are executed sequentially once a method starts executing. However, there are times when the execution of another method is what is desired. At such times, program flow is shifted from the method being executed to the method of interest through a method call (methods and data in a source code have identity or names so they can be called).

2.2.3 Conditional Transfer of Program Flow

Conditional Transfer of Program Flow is the transfer of program flow based on the result of a comparative analysis between two or more data. In this scenario, a method is called by the active method base on the satisfaction of a set condition.

2.2.4 Iteration or Looping

Iteration is the repetitive execution of a method (in the form of a block of consecutive instructions) based on specified criteria that consist of a start criterion, a test criterion that determines when to end the iteration and an action criterion. The criteria determine the number of loops. A loop is one-round of consecutive execution of the instructions in the block, beginning with the first instruction and ending with the last instruction.

2.2.5 Data Types and Structures

The data that methods act-upon are of various types and structures. These data are stored in data containers to which names and labels are assigned. The data containers whose contents vary are variables (their name may remain the same but the data they contain may vary).

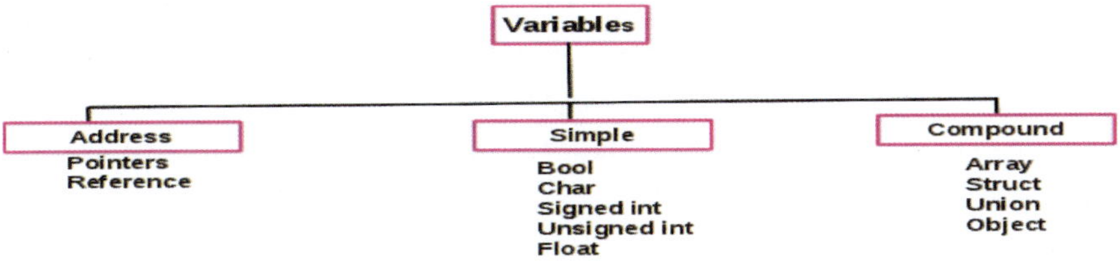

Figure. 2.1 Variable Types

The main data types are shown in figure 2.1. The data types are classified into three groups:

Simple variables which are single-value variables, that is, they contain just one value.

Address variables which are a special type of simple variables. The single value of an address variable is an address in main memory. They are called pointers in some programming languages.
Compound variables which are multi-value variables, that is, they contain more than one value which are usually the values of two or more simple variables.

The manner in which methods and data are expressed in a source code is dependent on the programming language being used. In general, source codes are written in High Level Programming Languages. These are languages that are more human friendly when compared to the machine language (coding in bits and bytes) that used to be the only language for writing source codes. Each High Level Programming Language has its syntax and semantics.

In 1955, FORTRAN (Formula Translator), created by John W. Backus (1924-2007), became the first modern high level programming language. Today, there are many high level programming languages: LISP, ALGOL, COBOL, APL, BASIC, PASCAL, C++, ADA, MATHLAB, PERL, PYTHON, HTML, RUBY, JAVA, JAVASCRIPT, PHP, etc. why so many languages? The simple answer to this question is that different people have different approaches to problem-solving. Essentially, each programming language has its advantages and disadvantages. A programmer selects a programming language based on its strength in the context of the problem he or she wants to solve. A programmer's selection may also be influenced by his or her likeness for a particular programming language. High Level Programming Languages allowed general purpose programs to be portable. It also gave programmers more flexibility in the manner in which they write their source codes.

2.2.6 Source Code to Machine Code

The *source code* cannot be executed by the computer because it is not written in *machine code*. The *interpreter* and the *compiler* are the computer programs used to transform the *source code* into an object code. The *interpreter* translates the *source code*, statement by statement and each statement it translates is then executed by the computer. But the *compiler* compiles the entire *source code* into an *object code* which is then handed to a linking program called a *linker*. The *linker* is responsible for combining all the object codes that constitute a program into executable machine code. Javascript and PHP programming languages (often called scripting languages), usually use interpreters to translate their source codes into executable codes. While programming languages like C, C++ use compilers to translate their source codes.
Many web applications are written in *scripting languages* because they are easy to learn and execute. But they are slower than compiled programs because of repetitive translation. A compiled program is compiled only once after which it can be executed as many times as needed.

Machine codes are strings of bits representing HIGH and LOW voltage states. This string of bits has two parts: the ***Opcode*** and the ***Operand***. The *Opcode* represents the machine instruction and the *operand* represents the data the instruction uses. The following is a machine code based on the machine codes of the intel X86 series of processor:

10100001 11111110 11000101 10100111 01010110
opcode -------------------- 32-bit------- value-------(operand)

The hexadecimal representation is:
A1 FE C5 A7 56

System Languages such as the Assembly Language were created to reduce the terseness of Machine Language. For example, in the Assembly Language, the *Opcode* is replaced by a mnemonic. An assemblage language has the following format:

Mnemonic destination operand, *source operand*.

For example, the following is an Assembly Language statement:

ADD EAX, EBX *(Both EAX and EBX are registers)*
In the above example*, ADD is the mnemonic, EAX* is the destination operand*, EBX* is the source operand.

2.3 Chapter summary

Software is an *algorithm* that can be executed by a computer. The set of the instructions that constitute the algorithm are coded using a high level programming language to create a *source code*. The source code is essentially groups of *methods* (also called *functions*) and the *data* the methods act-upon. The methods control the flow of the software. This flow is normally sequential unless it is changed by a *method call*, *conditional transfer* or an *iteration*. There are three basic groups of data types: *simple*, which are single-value variables; *address*, which are addresses of memory locations and *compound*, which consists of two or more simple data type.
Source codes are transformed into *machine codes* before they are executed inside the computer. The *interpreter*, *compiler* and *linker* are the computer programs used to transform source codes into machine executable codes.

3 Software Force

3.0 What is Force

A force is a *doer. It* makes things happen. This definition of *force* is consistent with the formal definition. According to physicists there are four fundamental forces in nature: the strong force, the weak force, electromagnetic force and gravity. All these forces are *doers*: the strong force holds the nucleus together against the tremendous force of the repulsion of the protons in the nucleus; the electromagnetic force holds atoms and molecules together; gravity exerts a pull on masses; and the weak force causes radioactive decay.

Software force, refers to the capacity of *software* as a *doer*. *Software force* is inherent in the electronic environment in which it works. In other words, *software* is able to solve the problems it was designed to solve because of the electronic circuitry inside the computer's processor. It does nothing without these circuits. The many *Integrated Circuits* (IC) that make up this circuitry have been translated into the ***Instruction Set*** (the machine codes) of the processor. *Software force* ultimately reduces to the *Instruction Set* of the processor within which it works. The I*nstruction Set* of a processor is dependent on its architecture. Nonetheless, in general, their conceptual role inside processors is constant.

3.1 Transistors

An Integrated Circuit (IC) is a large collection of individual electric and electronic circuits integrated on a silicon wafer. The ***Instruction Set*** of the processor is derived from the organization of the numerous ICs that constitute its internal circuitry. **Transistors** are the chief components of an integrated circuit. The number of transistors in an integrated circuit determines whether or not the circuit is Small Scale Integrated Circuit (SSIC) or Ultra Large Integrated Circuit (ULIC). A SSIC has few transistors while an ULIC can have several million transistors.

Transistors are *semi-conductors* of electricity. Electricity is fundamentally the result of the flow of electrons in a material. Materials that allow easy flow of electrons are called *conductors* while materials that disallow the flow of electrons are called *insulators*. A *semi-conductor* is a material that conducts electricity but not as well as a conductor. Silicon and Germanium are examples of semi-conductors.

Semi-conductors like silicon and germanium are *doped* before they can be used. *Doping* is the addition of impurities to the crystalline structure of a semi-conductor. It is used to control the number of charge carriers in a semiconductor. The impurity is called the *dopant.* It is either selected from group V or group III elements of the periodic table. Phosphorus and arsenic are examples of dopants from group V. Indium and gallium are examples of dopants from group III. When the dopant is a group V element, it is a *donor* because it gives a free electron to allow covalent bonding. When the dopant is a group III element, it is an *acceptor* because it accepts a free electron to allow covalent bonding.

Semiconductors doped with donor elements are called ***n-type*** semiconductors and they conduct electricity primarily by means of free electrons. Semiconductors doped with *acceptor* elements are called ***p-type*** semiconductors and they conduct current by means of holes.

Transistors are three-terminal semiconductors primarily made from either ***doped silicon*** or ***doped germanium.*** Transistors play two very important roles in electronic circuits: they are used to amplify signals and as electronic switches. The electronic switches of digital circuits are primarily transistors. Electronic amplification is the process of magnifying a signal by transferring energy to it from an external source. Electronic switching is the process of controlling a relatively large current or voltage between or across two terminals by means of a small control current or voltage applied at a third terminal.
There are two main types of transistors: **Bipolar Junction Transistors (BJT)** and **Field Effect Transistors (FET)**.

There are two types of Field Effect Transistors:
(1) **Junction Field Effect Transistors (JFET)**
(2) **Metal Oxide Semiconductor Field Effect transistors (MOSFET)** which consists of the ***enhancement mode MOSFET*** **and the *depletion mode MOSFET*.**

A *MOSFET* can be fabricated either as an ***n-Channel Metal Oxide Semiconductor Transistor*** **(nMOS)** or as a ***p-channel Metal Oxide Semiconductor*** **(pMOS).** In the *nMOS*, free electrons are the conductors while in the *pMOS*, *holes* are the conductors. The *switch-behavior* of *nMOS* and *pMOS* when voltage applied to its *gate* terminal is varied from a high voltage to a low voltage is why they are used as digital switches in digital circuits.

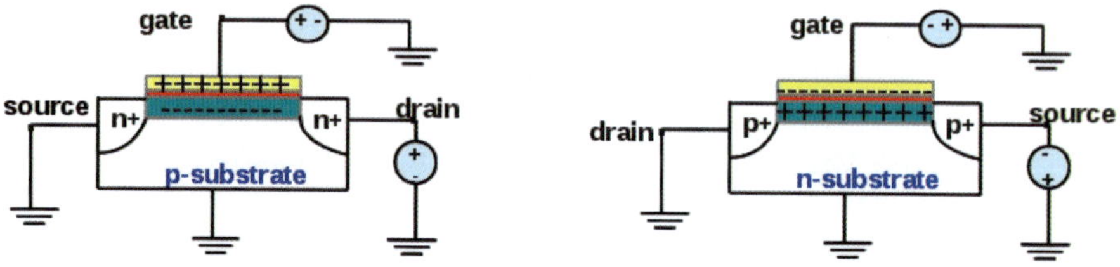

(a) gate voltage causes conducting n channel in nmos due to electrons.

Figure 3.4

(b) gate voltage causes conducting p channel in pmos due to holes.

Figure 3.4 is a diagram of a nMOS (3.4a) and a pMOS (3.4b). Each has three connection points: a ***source***, a ***drain***, and a ***gate***. Each has a silicon substrate and an insulating oxide layer that sits on top of it. Their topmost layer is ***polycrystalline silicon*** (called the *gate* because this layer used to be a metal).

The substrate of the *nMOS* has been doped with an *acceptor* element thereby leaving it positively charged. Its *source* and *drain* sections are a silicon substance that have been doped with a *donor* element and hence has excess electrons. The plus superscript indicates the concentration of doping. So, the *source* and *drain* terminals are equally well *doped* relative to the silicon substrate that separates them.

The substrate of the *pMOS* has been doped with an *a donor* element thereby leaving it negatively charged. Its *source* and *drain* sections are a silicon substance that have been doped with a *acceptor* element and hence has excess holes. The plus superscript indicates the concentration of doping. So, the *source* and *drain* terminals are equally well *doped* relative to the silicon substrate that separates them.

The nMOS behaves like a voltage-controlled-switch when an external voltage is applied to its gate. When a positive voltage is applied to its ***gate*****, e**lectrons from the silicon substrate are attracted to the transistor's *channel.*

These electrons collect at the channel without causing current to flow between the ***source*** and the ***drain*** until the *gate* voltage is higher than a pre-determined voltage called the Threshold Voltage (V_T), at which time enough electrons are pulled into the *channel* from the substrate and electrons flow across the transistor channel from the *source* to the *drain*. The nMOS is *on* at this state. If the voltage applied at the gate is zero or very small, little or no electrons flow through the channel from the *source* to the *drain*; that is, no current and the nMOS is *off* at this state. The conduction of electricity based on a HIGH voltage at the *gate* and the non-conduction of electricity based on a LOW voltage at the gate constitute the *switch mechanism* of the nMOS. A HIGH voltage implies the *switch* is ON and a LOW voltage implies the *switch* is OFF.

Figure 3.4b illustrates how the *pMOS* behaves differently from the *nMOS* when voltage is applied to its ***gate***. The silicon substrate is negatively charged while its ***source*** and ***drain*** sections are positively charged. When a negative voltage is applied to its gate, the charge carriers in the channel are no longer electrons but *holes* and the threshold voltage is negative, that is, $V_T < 0$. This scenario is the reverse of the switching characteristic of the nMOS. In other words, a HIGH voltage state at the *gate* of a pMOS transistor implies the pMOS is OFF and a LOW voltage state implies the pMOS is ON. Consequently, the nMOS and the pMOS are said to complement each other. So are called *Complementary Metal Oxide Semiconductors* (CMOS).

The nominal voltages of the HIGH and LOW voltage states depend on the design of the digital circuit. The mapping of the binary state 1 onto the HIGH voltage state of the transistor and the binary state 0 onto the LOW voltage state, makes it possible for binary INPUT-OUTPUT logic to be created in a digital circuit. This is why the inside of a processor is all about bits (1s and 0s), the binary digits of the binary number system.

The complementary nature of nMOS and pMOS, their low power consumption and the ease with which they can be fabricated make them very suitable for the design of ***integrated circuits***. Figure 3.5 shows the electronic symbols for the nMOS and the pMOS (has is a bubble at the gate terminal).

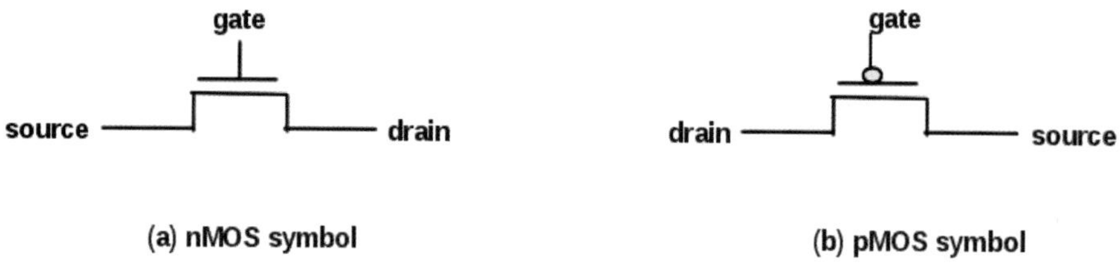

Figure 3.5

3.2 Logic Gates and Boolean Algebra

A ***logic gate*** is a specific arrangement of electronic components in a digital circuit that *outputs* either one of a binary state (1 or 0) when it receives one or more binary states as *inputs*. The nMOS and pMOS transistors are the electronic components commonly used to form *logic gates*. The INPUT-OUTPUT logic established by *logic gates* in a digital circuit is based on Bolean Algebra. *Boolean Algebra* was formulated by English mathematician and philosopher George Boole (1815-1864 AD). It has as its main operators, the conjunction **AND**, the disjunction **OR**, and the negation **NOT**. Other operators derived from these basic operators are: **NAND** which is the negation of AND; **NOR** which is the negation of OR; **XOR** which is exclusive OR (i.e. no more than one of the inputs is 1 for any given combination of the inputs) and **XNOR** which is exclusive NOR (the negation of NOR).

Basically, the objective of Boolean algebra is to determine the output for all possible combinations of a set of inputs when a given operator is applied to the inputs. All the possible combinations of the set of inputs and their respective outputs are indicated in a table called the **Truth Table**.

The NOT Gate

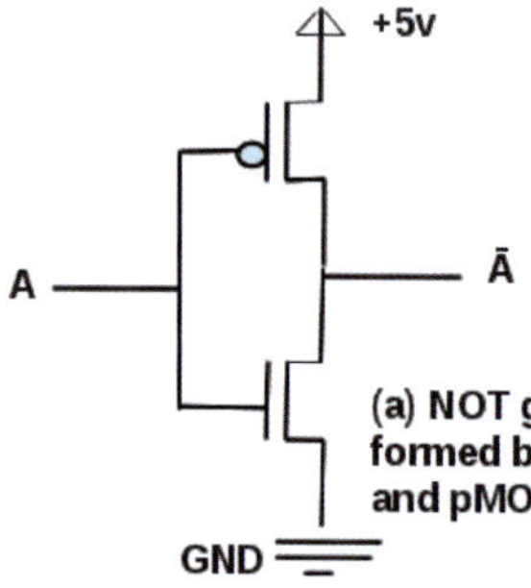

(a) NOT gate formed by nMOS and pMOS

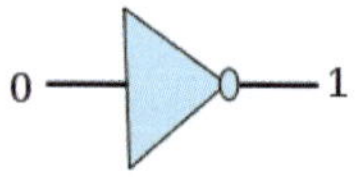

(b) NOT Gate/Inverter symbol

IN	OUT
0	1
1	0

(c) NOT- Truth Table

Figure 3.6

Figure 3.6a shows how a pMOS and a nMOS are connected in series to build a NOT gate. The pMOS *source* terminal is connected to a positive voltage supply while the *source* terminal of the nMOS is connected to ground. Figure 3.6b is the symbol for the NOT gate. The output = 1 for input A = 0 since current will flow from the pMOS to the output. There will be no current to the output from the nMOS since it is OFF for A = 0. When A = 1, there is no current from the pMOS since it is OFF when A=1. Also there is no current from the nMOS even though it is ON because it is connected to *ground*. So, the output = 0 when A = 1 as shown in the truth table (figure 3.6c). The NOT gate is also called an **INVERTER**.

The NAND Gate

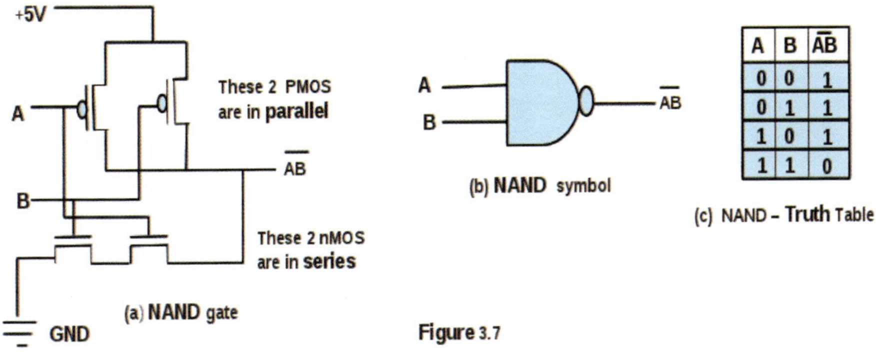

A	B	$\overline{AB}$
0	0	1
0	1	1
1	0	1
1	1	0

Figure 3.7

Figure 3.7a shows how two pMOS and two nMOS are connected to build a NAND gate. The pMOS are connected in parallel and the nMOS are connected in series. Figure 3.7b is the symbol for the NAND gate. When A = 0 and B = 0, there is a conduction path from each pMOS to the output. So the output=1. The output=1 whenever there is a conduction path from any of the pMOS to the output. The output=0 when there is no conduction path from any of the pMOS. This scenario occurs when A=1 and B=1 as shown in the truth table (figure 3.7c).

The NOR Gate

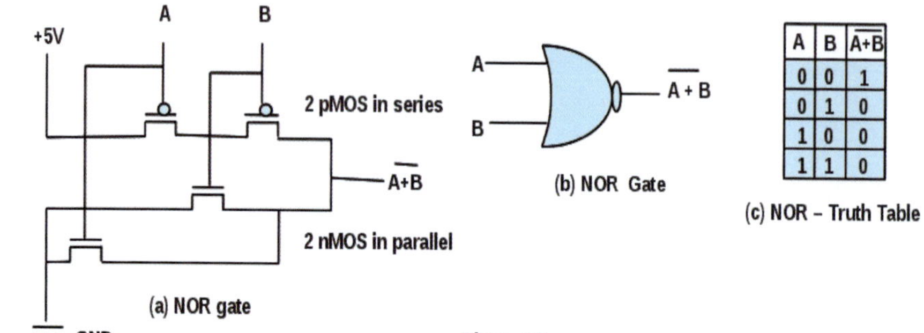

Figure 3.8

Figure 3.8a shows how two pMOS and two nMOS are connected to build a NOR gate. The pMOS are connected in series and the nMOS are connected in parallel. Figure 3.8b is the symbol for the NOR gate. When A = 0 and B = 0, there is a conduction path from each pMOS to the output. So the output = 1. The output is 0 for all other input values of A and B as shown in the truth table (figure 3.8c).

The AND Gate

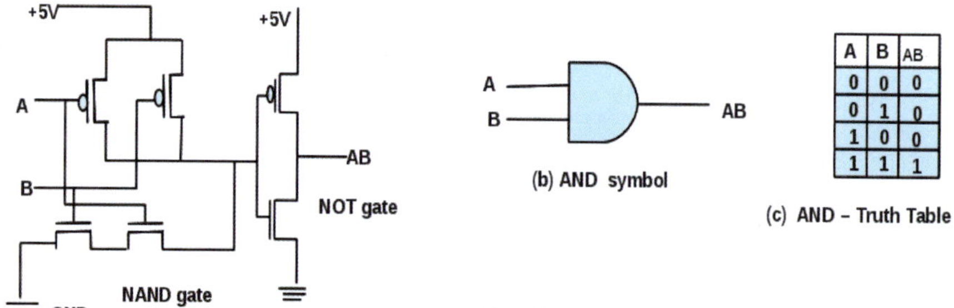

Figure 3.9

Figure 3.9a is an AND gate. In the diagram, the NAND gate is inverted by the NOT gate. Figure 3.9b is the symbol for the AND gate. The output=1 only when A=1 and B=1. The output=0 for all other input values as shown in the truth table (figure 3.9c).

The OR Gate

Figure 3.10a is an OR gate. In the diagram, the NOR gate is inverted by the NOT gate. Figure 3.10b is the symbol for

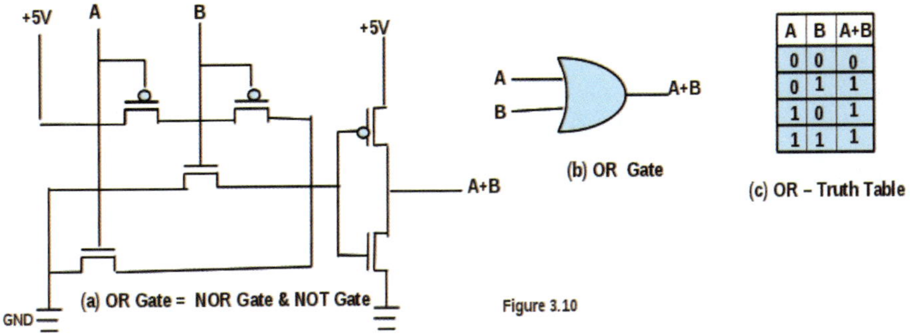

A	B	A+B
0	0	0
0	1	1
1	0	1
1	1	1

(a) OR Gate = NOR Gate & NOT Gate

(b) OR Gate

(c) OR – Truth Table

Figure 3.10

the OR gate. The output=1 when A=1 or B=1 or when A=1 and B=1. The output=0 for all other input values as shown in the truth table (figure 3.10c).

The XOR Gate

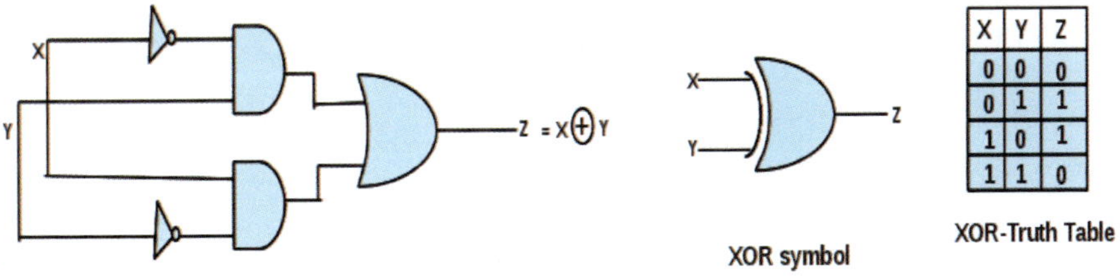

X	Y	Z
0	0	0
0	1	1
1	0	1
1	1	0

XOR symbol

XOR-Truth Table

(a) XOR (Exclusive OR) Gate

Also called EXOR Gate

Figure 3.11

Figure 3.11a is an XOR gate. Two NOT gates, two AND gates and an OR gate together build the XOR gate. Figure 3.11b is the symbol for the XOR gate. The output=1 when X=1 or Y=1. The output=0 for all other input values as shown in the Truth Table (Figure 3.11c).

In general, the pMOS transistors used to build logic gates are called Pull Up Network (PUN) because the *source* is typically connected to a voltage supply so that it can *pull-up* signals to realize the binary state 1 (logic 1).

The nMOS transistors are called Pull Down Network (PDN) because the *source* is typically connected to ground so that it can *pull-down* signals to realize the binary state 0 (logic 0).

Logic gates can be combined to build any number of gates with various degrees of complexities. In particular, NAND-gates and NOR gates. Consequently, some circuit technology uses the NAND-gate or NOR gate as the most primitive building block for digital circuits.

The Combination Circuits built from combining these logic gates form the digital circuitry of processor from which he Instruction Set is derived. Some examples of combinational circuits are the Multplexer, Demultiplexer, Full Adder, Encoder, Decoder, Comparator, etc. In general the goal of any logic gate design is to optimize the number of gates in the digital circuit taking into account the cost of fabrication and the desired functionality of the circuit. Important tools such as the Karnaugh Map (named after its inventor Karnaugh) and Hardware Description Languages are used for logic gate design optimization.

3.3 Chapter summary

Force is a doer. *Software force* is inherent in the *Instruction Set* of a processor. The *Instruction Set* of a processor is derived from its digital circuitry which is a composite of numerous *Integrated Circuits* (IC). These Integrated Circuits are Combinational Circuits built with Logic Gates. A *logic gate* is a specific arrangement of nMOS and pMOS that OUTPUTs either one of a binary state (1 or 0) when it receives one or more binary states as INPUT.

4 Software Motion

4.0 What is Motion

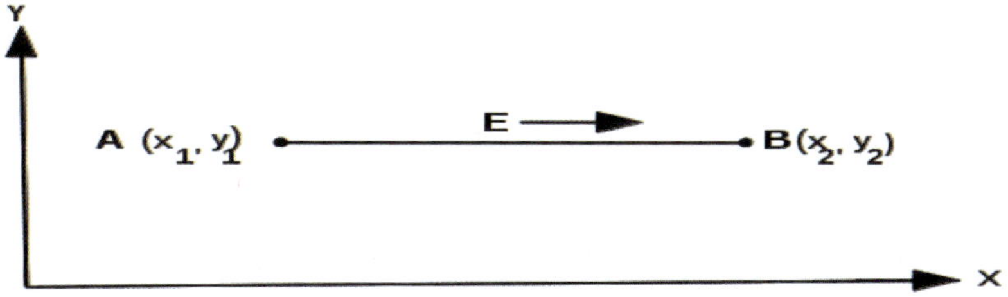

Figure 4.1 – The motion of E from A to B

Consider the points A and B in figure 4..1 and assume that the coordinates of **A** and **B** are (x_1, y_1) and (x_2, y_2) respectively, relative to a frame of reference in a given space. Suppose an entity **E** at A desires to get to **B**. The process by which **E** gets to **B** from **A** is called *motion*. In other words, *motion* is the process by which an entity changes its spatial position. *Motion* usually signifies a *time* differential because it is a continuum of different existential states; for example, the existential state of **E** at **A** is different from its existential state at **B**. The *Motion* of an entity is caused by the action of a *force* upon it. The entity moves from a position of rest when the magnitude of the force overcomes its inertia which is the entity's intrinsic resistance to motion due to its mass. The distance covered by the entity per unit time is called its speed or velocity. The entity moves at its speed uniformly unless a force is applied to it so as to vary its velocity. The rate of change of velocity per unit time is called *acceleration.*

Software motion is classified into two categories: *external software motion* which is the movement of *software* outside the *host* computer and *internal software motion* which is the movement of *software* inside the *host* computer.

4.1 External Software Motion

The functional existence of *software* begins in the computer. It remains in the computer unless it is removed by deletion or destruction of its host (the computer in which it resides).

Software motion occurs between unconnected computers through secondary storage devices and radio waves (figure 4.2). When a *software* in a particular computer is needed in another computer, it is copied onto a secondary storage device (CDs, Thumb Drives, etc) and moved to the computer that needs it. When both computers are part of a wireless connection (Wi-Fi), software can be moved through radio waves. For example, the wireless technology called *bluetooth* can move *software* to and from two computers that contain the *bluetooth* technology and are at a limited distance apart. The *external motion* of *software* in computers that are part of a wired network, occurs through the cables that connect the computers. The *software* in computers that are part of a network can be functional during its *external motion*; for example, in a computer network the *software* in one of the computers in the network can be used to implement an event in another computer.

4.2 Internal Software Motion

In chapter 2, we identified software as being a collection of instructions which are essentially *methods* acting upon *data*. *Internal software motion* refers to how these *methods* and *data* are moved within the computer. The space where this internal motion occurs is the software's *workspace*, that is, its *dynamic space*.

4.2.1 The Dynamic Space of software

The computing space of the computer can be conceptually represented by the spaces illustrated in figure 4.3.

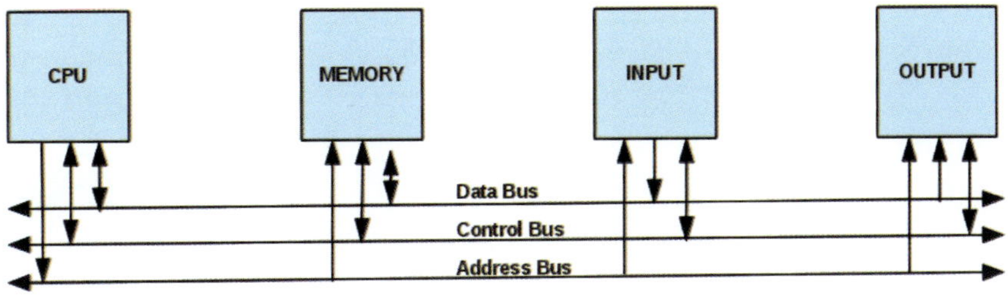

Figure 4.3 – Basic Computer Architecture

In figure 4.3, the CPU block represents the space inside the processor, that is, the Central Processor Unit. The Memory block represents the Random Access Memory (RAM). The Input block represents input devices such as the keyboard, mouse, sensors, secondary storage devices (Optical and magnetic disks) and other computers. The Output block represents output devices such as the monitor, printer, storage devices (Optical disks and hard disks) and other computers. The *buses* are signal paths. Figure 4.3 shows that all the spaces interact with the control bus that transmit control signals. The CPU and Memory spaces have a two-way signal flow with the data bus. They receive and put data on the data bus. The Input and Output spaces have a one-way signal flow with the data bus. The Input space puts data on the data bus while the Output space receives data from the data bus. The CPU is the only space that puts address signals on the address bus. The other spaces receive address signals from the address bus. The **Central Processing Unit (CPU)**, **Memory** and **Buses** constitute the dynamic space of software. Traffic on the buses is controlled by *chipsets* or *controllers*.

The Central Processing Unit (CPU)

The Central Processing Unit is usually called the brain of the computer. Its primary resident is the processor. The processor's primary task is to process the instructions and data submitted to it and then send the result to the appropriate output. The *Control Uni*t which coordinates the processing with the help of a clock, the *Arithmetic and Logic Unit (ALU)* which is responsible for the arithmetic and logic tasks of the computer and used by the CPU to temporarily hold data are also part of the central processing unit. Figure 4.4 is a conceptual view of the CPU's key spaces.

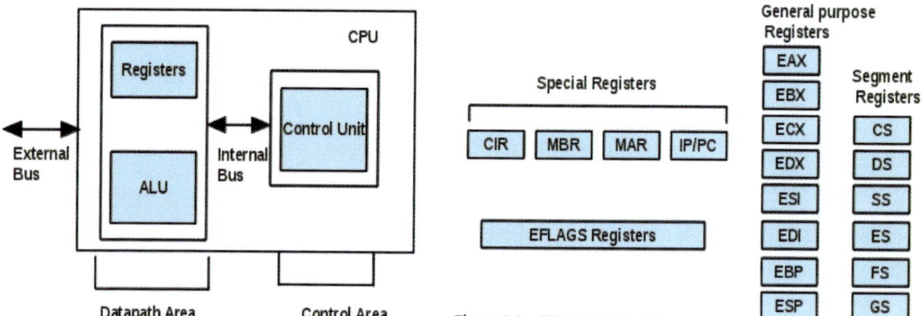

Figure 4.4 – CPU Components

The **Arithmetic and Logic Unit** (ALU) is where all the arithmetic and logic computations take place. The *Arithmetic functions* are carried-out by *adder* and *subtractor* circuits while the *logic functions* are implemented by *comparator* circuits. The ALU uses the general purpose registers to carry-out its computations.

The **Special Registers** are: the *Memory Address Register (MAR,* holds main memory address); the bi-directional Memory Buffer Register (MBR, holds data fetched from memory or data waiting to be stored in memory); the *Current Instruction Register (CIR,* holds current instruction); the Instruction *Pointer or Program Counter* (IP/PC, points to the next instruction to be fetched).

The **General-Purpose Registers** are used to hold data for logical and arithmetic operations, operands for address calculations and memory pointers. The specific functions of these registers are as follows:

(1) The **EAX** register, also called the accumulator, is used to hold results from the ALU. Operations, such as MUL (multiply) and DIV (divide), require that one of the operands be in the accumulator. Operations, such as ADD (addition) and SUB (subtraction), do not mandate the involvement of the *accumulator*. However, the operation of ADD and SUB are more conveniently carried-out if the EAX register is involved in the operation.

(2) The **EBX** register is used to hold the pointer to the the Data Segment (DS) of a segmented memory space. It is a *base* register and the only general purpose register which may be used for *indirect addresssing*. For example, the instruction *MOV [EBX], EAX* causes the contents of EAX to be stored in the memory location whose address is given in EBX.

(3) The **ECX** register is used as a counter for string and loop operations. The looping instructions, the shift and rotate instructions and the string instructions, use the ECX register to determine the required number of repetitions.

(4) The **EDX** register is used with the EAX register for MUL and DIV operations. Also it holds the port number for the IN and OUT instructions. In general, it is used for temporary storage of data just like all the other general-purpose registers.

(5) The **ESI** register is used as a pointer to data in the segment pointed to by the DS register and as a source pointer for string operations. All string operations use the ESI register as the source-operand pointer.

(6) The **EDI** register is used as a pointer to data in the segment pointed to by the ES register and as a destination-operand pointer for string operations.

(7) The **EBP** register is used as a pointer to data on the stack (in the SS segment). It is a *base* pointer which can be used for indirect addressing in a way similar to how EBX is used.

(8) The **ESP** register is a stack pointer. It indicates the current position of the top of the stack.

The six **Segment Registers** are: *Code Segment (CS)* register, *Stack Segment (SS)* register and data segment registers (DS, ES, FS and GS). These registers provide flexible and efficient access to the instructions and data in memory. A *segment selector* is a special pointer that identifies a segment in memory. The three memory segments are: the *code segment*, the *data segment* and the *stack segment* (the stack is a temporary holding place for instructions and data). Modern *software* does not use the segmented memory model. Instead, it uses the (unsegmented) whereby memory is referenced as a single linear-address space.

The **Eflag Register** is a 32-bit register that provides status and control for basic arithmetic, compare, and system operations.

Memory

Random Access Memory (RAM) is the next major space of the *dynamic space* of software. Its primary function is to provide temporary residence for the instructions and data that constitute *software* and the results of the executions of the instructions. The storage is temporary because contents of RAM are lost when its source of power is turned off. Hence RAM is called *volatile* memory.

RAM's primary characteristics of interest are its storage capacity (measured in bytes) and its speed (measured in hertz). A byte is 8 bits (a bit is a 0 or a 1). In memory storage:
One Kilobyte (1K) = 1024 bytes;
one Megabyte (1M) = 1024 Kilobytes;
One Gigabyte (1G) = 1024 Megabytes
One Terabyte (1T) = 1024 Gigabytes.

The effective RAM memory in the *dynamic space* of *software* is the *addressable memory of RAM.* The *addressable memory of RAM* is a function of the width of the address bus of a processor. Common address bus width are 32 bits and 64 bits, an improvement on the address bus widths of 8 bits and 16 bits of earlier processors. In general, the addressable memory of RAM is $\mathbf{2^n}$ where *n* is the address bus width.

RAM's speed is measured in Hertz. A Hertz is one cycle per second. A RAM's cycle is the start to finish of a read/write operation. A RAM's speed of 100MHz implies that the RAM can carry out 100 Million read/write operations in one second (here Mega = 100,000,000).

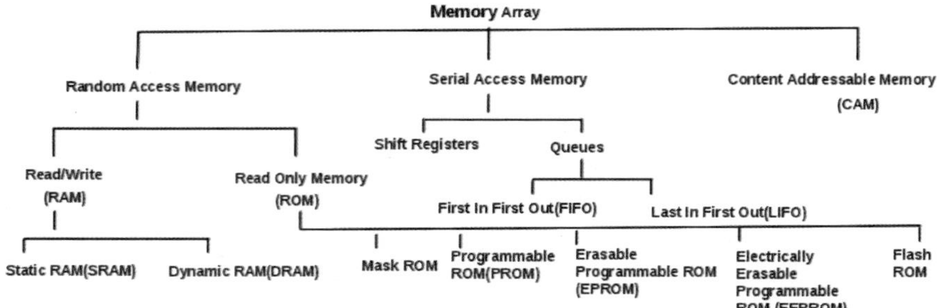

Figure 4.5

Figure 4.5 shows the different types of commonly used memories. It shows that there are two types of Random Access Memory: ***Read/Write*** *Random Access Memory* (RAM) and **Read Only Memory** (ROM). The former can be read from and written onto while the latter can only be read from. ROMs are usually the memory used for the *Basic Input/Output System* (BIOS) of the processor. The BIOS are responsible for the initial start up processes of the computers.

RAM is further classified into two types: **Static Random Access Memory** (SRAM) and **Dynamic Random Access Memory** (DRAM). The **memory cells** (the memory unit) of both types of memory are made from pMOS and nMOS transistors. SRAM is made from either two pMOS and four nMOS (6-Tcell) arrangement or the two pMOS and two nMOS (4 -Tcell) arrangement. DRAM is made from a single nMOS connected to a capacitor which is referenced to a power source for charging or to Ground for discharging. The capacitor is either charged or discharged; these two states are used to represent the two binary states, 0 and 1. The charged capacitor leaks its charge because of the sub-threshold current of the cell transistor. So, the capacitor is recharged several times each second. DRAM memory cells are arranged in a rectangular array to form a memory *core*. DRAM is smaller, slower and less expensive than SRAM. DRAM is small because it has only one transistor. It is slower than SRAM because its capacitor discharges quickly and has to be recharged or *refreshed* periodically (DRAM is called *dynamic* because of this refresh process). DRAM is cheaper than SRAM because of its single-tansistor design.

DRAMs are the main memories of personal computers and workstations. Cache memories and other speed-sensitive applications use SRAMs. DRAMs have evolved over the years. Their evolution has primarily been in the direction of memory capacity and speed. In the early days of personal computers (1980s), DRAM capacity was often expressed in kilobytes. Today, DRAM capacity of 1 GigaBytes (GB) or more is common. Memory speed in the Mega Hertz (MHz) is also common.

The following are some types of DRAMs:
Fast Page DRAM (FPDRAM): introduced in 1987. It allows multiple accesses to a memory location with just a single specification of the location's address.

Extended Data Output RAM (EDO): introduced in 1990. It is about 10% faster than Fast Page DRAM and uses assumptions about the next memory access to pre-read data. It is sometimes called Hyper Page Mode (HPM) DRAM.
Single Data-Rate Synchronous Dynamic Random Access Memory (SDR-SDRAM): introduced in 1997. SDR-SDRAM replaced the traditional Asynchronous Dynamic Random Memory (ASDRAM). ASDRAM became too slow because it did not operate in sync with the processor. SDRAM improved memory speed by synchronizing memory responses to control inputs with the system bus clock.
RAMBUS: introduced in 1999. It is based on a type of video memory and designed for use in PCs with Intel pentium processors.
RAMBUS DRAM (RDRAM): improved version of RAMBUS designed to operate at faster bus speeds of up to 800MH.
Double Data Rate SDRAM (DDR-SDRAM)): introduced in 2000. Data can be transferred on both the rising and falling edges of the clock signal. Therefore, data is moved nearly twice as quickly as with regular SDR SDRAM. Also memory runs at a lower clock rate (100-200MHz) and uses less energy.
Double Data Rate2 SDRAM (DDR2-SDRAM): introduced in 2004. Faster than DDR and uses less energy. **Double Data Rate3 SDRAM** (DDR3-SDRAM): introduced in 2007. Faster than DDR2 and consumes less energy.

Buses

The computer **bus** is a data pathway used by the components of a computer to communicate with one another or with the components in another computer. Buses are usually physical (cable, wire, electronic prints, etc) connections between components and are designed to optimize the number of paths needed for communication among components. Some connections are non-physical, for example, a socket connection in a network is a software connection. A *bus* is called a *port* if only two components use it to communicate with each other. The *serial port* transmits via a single bus while the *parallel port* transmits via two or more buses.

The width of a bus is determined by the number of physical lines it has for the transmission of bits. For example, a 32-wire bus can transfer 32 bits in parallel. The speed of a bus measures how fast the bits flow per second. It is denoted as the frequency of the bus and is measured in Hertz. The number of bits a bus can transmit per second or its data transfer rate is called its *bandwidth*.

In reality, a bus is generally made up of 50 to 100 distinct physical lines which are divided into three sub assemblies:
(1) The *address bus:* unidirectional and transports memory addresses for processor's read/write operation.
(2) The *data bus:* bidirectional and transports instructions and data.
(3) The *control bus:* bidirectional and transports control signals to various components in the computer.

4.2.2 The Fetch Decode Execute Cycle

Internal software motion in the *dynamic space* of *software* consists almost entirely of the movements of *software instructions* and *data*. These movements can be conceptually grouped as follows:
(1) Memory to Register
(2) Register to Memory
(3) Register to Register
(4) Immediate data to Memory
(5) Immediate data to Register
(6) Memory to Input/Output
(7) Register to Input/Output
(8) Immediate data to Input/Output.

These movements occur contextually during the computing cycle known as **The Fetch-Decode-Execute Cycle**.

The Fetch Phase of The Fetch-Decode-Execute Cycle

The first instruction fetch is implemented by the Basic Input/Output System (BIOS). However, this fetch is not usually considered to be part of the fetch phase of the standard Fetch-Decode-Execute Cycle . The BIOS is a special type of software that resides permanently in the Read Only Memory (ROM) of the computer. It has several important functions most of which has to do with preparing the computer for normal operations; for example, the BIOS is responsible for checking the circuits of the system board and the memory, the keyboard, the disks and each expansion board, and is in control of all the activities involved in Power-On-Self-Test (POST). However, the BIOS activity that is considered as the first instruction fetch in this presentation, is the loading of the operating system (system software) into main memory. Once the BIOS loads the operating system, it hands over control to the operating system. The operating system then loads the application software into main memory, and places the address of the first instruction of the application software in the *Instruction Pointer (IP)* register. The Instruction Pointer is also called the ***Program Counter** (PC).*

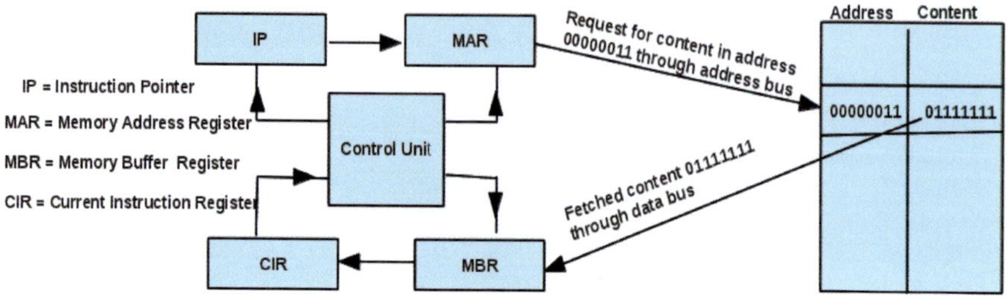

Figure 4.6 – The Fetchphase of
The Fetch-Decode-Execute Cycle

Figure 4.6 is an illustration of the fetch sequence of the fetch phase. It begins when the control unit signals that the instruction pointed to by the Instruction Pointer be fetched. The memory address in the Instruction Pointer is placed in the Memory Address Register (MAR) from where it is sent to main memory (DRAM) via the address bus. Main Memory then puts the instruction on the data bus. The instruction is received in the CPU by the Memory Buffer Register (MBR) and then passed to the Current Instruction Register (CIR) where it will be decoded by the control unit. The arrival of the instruction at the Current Instruction Register marks the end of an instruction fetch sequence. The content of the Instruction Pointer is then incremented to indicate the address of the next instruction to be fetched.

The Decode Phase of The Fetch-Decode-Execute Cycle

The control unit decodes the fetched instruction in the Current Instruction Register during this phase. The control unit's objective is to determine the control sequence of the machine instruction represented by the *opcode* of the fetched instruction. This information has been encoded in the *Instruction Format* associated with the processor. The Instruction Format maps the machine instruction (opcode) with the control sequence assigned to the opcode.

The Execute Phase of The Fetch-Decode-Execute Cycle

The *execute phase* simply implements the results of the *decode phase*. The *control unit* sends out control signals to the *function unit (ALU)* and other areas of the *datapath* as necessary to implement the decoded *machine instruction*.

Execution of a *machine instruction* involves several *micro-operations*. In general, the task performed by any micro-operation can be grouped as follows:
Data transfer from one register to another register;
Register to an external interface (system bus) data transfer;
External interface to register data transfer;
Arithmetic or logic operations, using registers for input and output.

4.3 Chapter Summary

Motion is the process by which an entity changes its spatial position.

There are two types of software motions: *external software motion* and *internal software motion*. *External software motion* is the movement of software outside its host computers. *Internal software motion* is the movement of software within computers.

The control unit inside the CPU controls internal software motion.
Fundamentally, internal software motion is a Fetch-Decode-Execute Cycle.
During the fetch phase of the Fetch-Decode-Execute Cycle, the Memory Address Register (MAR) requests the instruction in the memory address pointed to by the Instruction Pointer (IP) through the address bus; main memory places instruction on the data bus; the Memory Buffer Register (MBR) receives instruction and directs it to the Current Instruction Register (CIR) where it is decoded by the control unit.

During the decode phase of the Fetch-Decode-Execute Cycle, the fetched instruction in the Current Instruction Register is translated into a machine instruction according to the Instruction Format of the processor.

During the execute phase of the Fetch-Decode-Execute Cycle, the control unit sends control signals to the appropriate areas of the datapath for execution; for example, arithmetic and logic calculations are sent to the Arithmetic and Logic Unit for execution.

Generally, internal software motion consists of:
Movement of instructions from main memory to register
Movement of data between memory and registers
Movement of data between registers
Movement of data between I/O and memory
Movement of data within register (bits shift and rotations)

5 Software Change

5.0 What is Change?

Consider the following familiar experiences: walking then running; standing then sitting; sleeping then waking up. We see in each of these three experiences, two mutually exclusive states and a transition from one state to the other; for example, an entity can not walk and run at the same time. It must transit from the walk-state to the run-state. In essence, *change* is the transition from one existential state to another existential state given that both states are mutually exclusive, that is, both states can not exist at the same time. Let us examine another example of change that is not as obvious as the preceding examples.

Suppose a driver parks his car in a parking lot. Then a thief comes and steals the stereo equipment in the car. Definitely, the states of the car before and after the theft are mutually exclusive. In other words, the state of the car with its stereo intact is existentially different from the state without the stereo after the theft (both states can not co-exist). Therefore, change has occured with respect to the state of the car. The agent of this change is the thief and the car without its stereo is a changed-state.

The mutual exclusivity criterion for change as illustrated in the preceding examples applies to the strict definition of change. It is diluted when applied to the concept of software change because software is an intellectual abstraction. Once the stereo in the car example was stolen, the existential state of the car was changed.

The car with its stereo intact no longer exists. In the software space both the changed software and the software that is the object of change can co-exist albeit not exactly in the same space. This is accomplished by making a copy of the software to be changed. So in this presentation, software change does not imply strict mutual exclusivity. However, it does imply a change in existential state.

5.1 Sources of Software Change

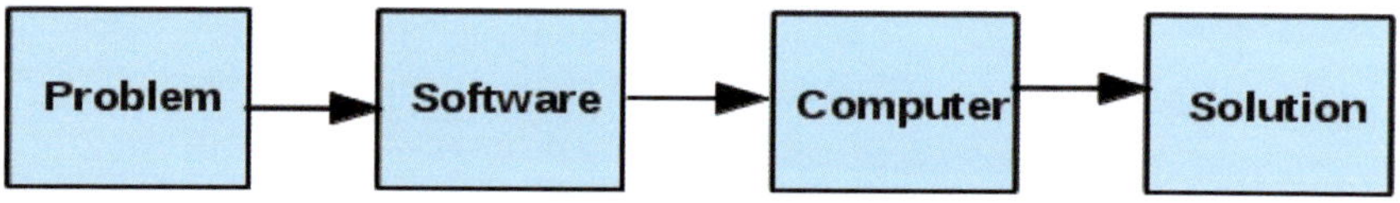

Figure 5.1 - Software's Objective

In chapters 2 we established that *software* is essentially constituted by *instructions* and the *data* the instructions act-upon. The objective is to use these instructions and data to solve a specific problem using the computer. This objective is summarized in figure 5.1. Figure 5.1 illustrates the *software concept*: a problem is defined by humans and *software* is created to solve the problem. The *software* is submitted to a computer for processing. If all goes well, the computer processes the *software* and outputs the solution. It is easy to see the sources of *software change* from figure 5.1. If the problem changes, *software* will change; if the environment in which *software* is processed changes, *software* will change and if during their interaction with *software's* solution, users discover important needs not addressed in the solution, *software* will change. These *software change* scenarios can be formally classified into four types: *corrective change*, *adaptive change*, *perfective change* and *preventive change*. These changes are initiated by modification requests which have been broadly classified into two types: *corrective* and *enhancement*.

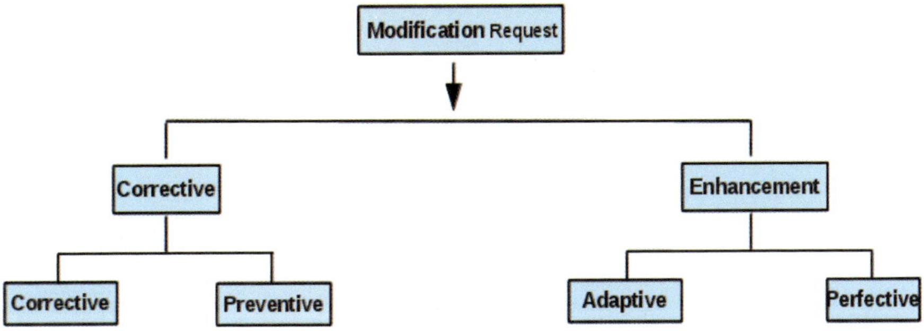

Figure 5.2 – Software Change

Figure 5.2 illustrates the software changes classified under the two primary modification requests: *corrective* and *enhancement*. It is assumed in this presentation that the *software* has been deployed and it is operational.

5.1.1 Corrective Change

Corrective Software Change is made to correct errors, faults or defects discovered during the operation of the software. The errors can be any or all of the following: design errors, logic errors and coding errors. Design and logic errors are caused by incorrect understanding and definition of the problem and therefore incorrect programming specifications. Coding errors are caused by wrong interpretation of problem algorithm. Other errors include data processing errors and system performance errors. These errors are often called *residual errors* or *bugs* and they prevent the proper operation of the software. Sometimes, quick fixes of these errors are implemented with *patches*. A patch is a piece of software created to fix specific software errors. A poorly designed patch can cause future problems for the software it is supposed to fix.

5.1.2 Adaptive Change

Adaptive Software Change is made to a software that is operational because of changes that occur in its operational environment. So even in the absence of residual errors, software is bound to change because the socio-economic and political environments in which it operates are always changing. For example, software often adapts to changes in business rules, government policies and work patterns; and to new hardware and operating system technologies.

A good example of how government policies result in *adaptive software change* occurred when several European countries formed the European Union and adopted the Euro as their currency. The adoption of the Euro caused government and business software systems of these countries to adapt to the new financial infra-structure. Another example was the Year 2000 software change.

The technological advances of computer processors present good examples of how advances in technology result in *adaptive software change*. In 1978, Intel introduced its 8086 processor. This chip was a 16-bit processor and it communicated with its cards through a 16 wire data connection. The chip's 29,000 transistors and 20 address lines made a 1 MB RAM possible. The chip designers never suspected that anyone would ever need more than 1 MB of RAM space. There were 5, 6, 8 and 10 MHz versions of the 8086 processor. This Intel 8086 processor never became as popular as the Intel 8088 processor which was introduced in 1979. The intel 8088 processor was identical to the 8086. It was different only in the format of its addressing mode. However, the Intel 8088 processor became popular because it was the processor chosen by IBM for the first IBM PC. Today, processors with GigaHertz speeds, GigaBytes RAM and 32-bit or 64-bit data busses are commonly available. *Software* has continually adapted to these technological changes.

5.1.3 Perfective Change

Perfective Change is the change towards perfect software functionality. *Perfective Change* is usually a function of a *software's* success. As a *software* achieves operational success, users experiment with various scenarios beyond the scope of the original design of the software. The requests and desires users express as a result of their interaction with the *software* are usually sources for enhancement ideas that often develop to enhance the functionality of the *software. Perfective change i*s usually incremental. In other words, the *change* is incorporated into new releases of the software.

5.1.4 Preventive Change

Preventive Change is the change made to software in order to prevent future software malfunctions that can result from the structural complexities caused by the quick fixes of the software's residual errors. The change is usually effected with the intention of making the software easier to understand. The gain in baseline functionality due to preventive change is usually minimal.

Some of the ways in which preventive change is implemented include: code restructuring, code optimization and documentation updating. Code restructuring addresses the structural complexities caused by series of quick fixes of the software's residual errors. Code optimization takes advantage of the capabilities of the hardware that runs the software so as to improve the speed and general performance of the software. Documentation Updating allows users to be aware of the current state of the software, that is, users are informed about the changes made to the software so as to prevent user mistakes caused by lack of information on the change-state of the software.

5.2 Implementation of Software Change

Software like any other human creation requires maintenance. The objective of any maintenance team is to sustain and if possible improve the object that is being maintained. As a result those who maintain software are usually required to understand the software they are maintaining. The number of maintenance personnel assigned to maintain a given software depends on the complexity of the software. Complex software such as E-type systems which are elaborate software used in the real world by governments and large corporations usually require a well-staffed maintenance team. Maintenance personnel implement software changes.

The importance of software maintenance and evolution was first articulated by mathematician and computer scientist Meir Manny Lehman (1925-2010) in association with computer scientist Laszlo Belady (1928 -). Lehman's research in software maintenance and evolution spanned 20 years and resulted in the group of eight software evolution principles he called Lehman Laws. Over the years, these laws have provided beneficial insight into the understanding of software maintenance and evolution.

Fundamentally, Lehman's Laws enunciate the importance of adapting software to its ever changing environment; the importance of reducing the structural complexities caused by such adaptations and the important role played by feedback in software maintenance and evolution.

5.3 Chapter Summary

Change is the transition from one existential state to another existential state given that both states are mutually exclusive. This *mutual exclusivity* criterion is relaxed in the case of *software change* because the *software* that is *changed* can co-exists with its replacement in the same conatainer.

There are four basic types of *software change*:
corrrective change, *adaptive change*, *perfective change* and *preventive change*.

Software maintenance is a very important part of the life-cycle of *software*. The maintainers of *software* are the implementers of *software changes*. In many instances, the maintainers of *software* are also its developers.

Lehman Laws have provided beneficial insight into the understanding of software maintenance and evolution.

6 Software Grouping/Interaction

6.0 What is Grouping?

A *group* is a collection of entities with one or more similar characteristics. *Grouping* is the act of forming a group. The characteristics used to select members of a group defines the group and must be common to all members of the group; for example, the periodic table groups elements according to their *valence electrons*, that is, the number of electrons in their outer shells. Some other important groups are: *vertebrates* (animals with backbones), *invertebrates* (animals without backbones), electric conductors, semiconductors, insulators, etc. The number of possible groups are probably uncountable.

6.1 Software Groups

Software can be broadly classified into two groups: *Application Software* and *System Software* (figure 6.1).

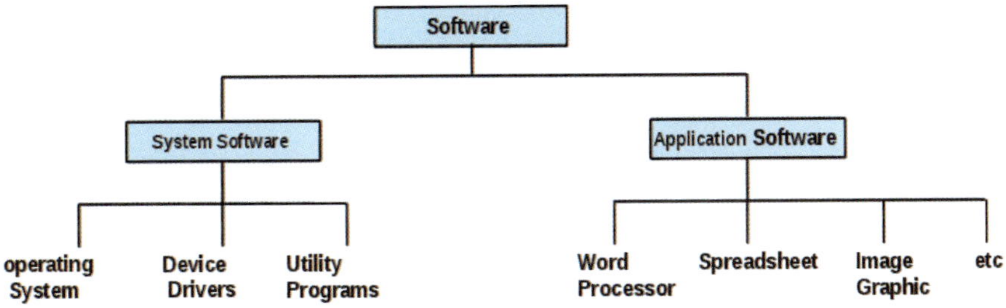

Figure 6.1

An application software solves a specific problem for its users; for example, a word processor is an application software that allows its users to create documents; an image/graphics software is an application software that allows its users to draw and edit images; a spreadsheet is an application software that allows its users to carry-out calculations on data entered in cells formed by the intersection of horizontal and vertical lines.

A System Software is a collection of software that manage and coordinate hardware and application software activities. System Software broadly consists of three types of software: operating system (the kernel), utility programs (programs that fix specific hardware and software problems) and device drivers (programs that describe how hardware devices operate).

6.1.1 The Operating System

The key functions of the operating system are:
(1) *User Interface Management*: this function allows users to access and use the application programs and utility programs in the computer; for example, if a user wants to Load an application software, he or she calls the operating system to load the application software into memory (RAM). The operating system provides a *user interface* in both a graphical format (GUI) and a text format.
(2) *Application Program Interface (API)*: this function provides some degree of hardware independence because the operating system provides a layer between the application software and the hardware. Consequently, the same application software can be used on various hardware, that is, the software is *portable*.
(3) Device Management: if an application software wants the services of an input/output device, it calls the operating system. The operating system calls the device driver of the device and both make sure that the input/output device is available to the application software. The device driver must be available for the input/output device to work.

(4) Management of File System: the operating system stores and organizes all files in a directory format on both primary and secondary storage devices. It retrieves files when they are needed and deletes files that are no longer needed.(5) Memory Management: the operating system manages memory on behalf of the application software. It keeps track of used and unused memory spaces and ensures that both codes and data are stored in their appropriate spaces in memory.

(6) Process Management: in multitasking environments, the CPU is able to carry-out multiple tasks or processes. The operating system allocates CPU time to processes according to priorities. When the end of the CPU time allocated to a process has elapsed, the process is stopped and the operating system hands over the CPU to the next process. This allocation of CPU time is called scheduling. The operating system also facilitates communication between processes and ensures that the security of processes is not compromised. In other words, it keeps track of each process, process ownership and the operating environment of each process and ensures that no process arbitrarily accesses the operating environment of another process.

(7) Conflict Management: sometimes an event occurs at an input/output device that interrupts the current task of the CPU. Such an event is called a hardware interrupt. The interrupt causes a signal to be sent from the input/output device through an interrupt-request (IRQ) line in the system bus to the CPU. When the CPU receives the signal, it finishes its current instruction and then calls the operating system to attend to the interrupt. The operating system in association with the device driver for the device, resolves the interrupt and returns execution control to the CPU at the point at which it was interrupted.

6.1.2 Utility Programs

Utility programs are used to carry-out specific functions that enhance hardware and software operations. The following are some important utility programs:
(1) *Anti-virus utilities*: scan for computer viruses.
(2) *Backup utilities*: create backup copies of information stored on a disk and can restore the entire disk content or some selected files in the event of a disk failure.
(3) *Cryptography utilities*: encrypt streams (strings of bytes) and files.
(4) *Data compression utilities*: reduce the size of streams and files.
(5) *Disk compression utilities*: can compress the contents of a disk.
(6) *Disk defragmenter utilities*: increase storage efficiency by rearranging files whose contents are stored in various locations on a hard disk.
(7) *Disk partition utilities*: partition individual drive.
(8) *System monitor utilities*: monitor resources and performance in a computer system.
(9) *System profile utilities*: provide detailed information about the software installed and hardware attached to the computer.
(10) *Network utilities*: analyze the computer's network connectivity, configure network settings, check data transfer or log events.

6.1.3 Device Drivers

A device driver is a software that provides the hardware interface needed to initialize and manage the operation of a specific hardware. Iit is the device driver that the operating system calls upon when an application software needs access to the hardware. There are two types of device drivers: *architecture-specific drivers* and *generic drivers*.

(1) ***Architecture-Specific Drivers***: these drivers initialize and enable CPU components such as on-chip memory, memory management units (MMU) and floating-point hardware (also known as math co-processor).
(2) ***Generic Drivers***: these drivers initialize and manage hardware connected to the motherboard that are not integrated into the processor; for example, motherboard buses, DRAM and I/O devices (monitor, mouse, printer, network cards, etc) are managed by generic device drivers. Some aspects of device drivers codes are architecture-specific since all processes are controlled by the processor. However, generic device drivers are essentially processor independent.

A device driver is usually written to manage a specific hardware, that is, its function is hardware specific. However, in general, all device drivers have in common all or a subset of the following twelve functions:
(1) *Hardware Startup*: initializes hardware upon PowerON or reset.
(2) *Hardware Shutdown*: configures hardware into its PowerOFF state.
(3) *Hardware Disable*: permits another software to disable hardware.
(4) *Hardware Enable*: permits another software to enable hardware.
(5) *Hardware Acquire*: permits another software to gain singular (locking) access to hardware.
(6) *Hardware Release*: permits another software to free (unlock) hardware.
(7) *Hardware Read*: permits another software to read data from hardware.
(8) *Hardware Write*: permits another software to write data to hardware.
(9) *Hardware Install*: permits another software to install new hardware
(10) *Hardware Uninstall:* permits another software to remove installed hardware.

(11) *Hardware Mapping*: permits address mapping of hardware storage devices for read/write or delete operations.
(12) *Hardware Unmapping*: permits removal of data blocks from hardware storage devices.

The existential states of any hardware consist of an *inactive state*, an *active state* and *transition states* into and out of the two preceding states. The design of device drivers is based on hardware states. For instance, a hardware that is *inactive* can be perceived as either disconnected, without power or disabled. So, the design could employ the Install function to connect the hardware, or the PowerON initialization routine to turn on the hardware, or the Enable routine to enable the hardware. Similarly, the Uninstall, Shutdown and/or Disable functions could be employed to disconnect a hardware that is *active*.

6.2 What is Interaction?

An *Interaction* is the *action-reaction* state between two or more entities. An interaction may or may not involve physical contact between the entities. However, it always has the following components: ***actions-initiators*** (the entities that began the interaction) and ***actions-responders*** (the entities that respond to the actions). All Interactions are ***active associations***. Therefore, all interactions are subject to the ***Association Principle*** which states that *there is at least one reason for an active association and at least one result from the association*. Also, the *Association Principle* broadly categorizes associations into three groups: *human-human association*, *human-thing* association and *thing-thing* association. Some examples of interactions include communications between two or more people (human-human association); communication between a computer user and the computer (human-thing association); communication between computers (thing-thing association).

6.3 Software Interactions

6.3.1 The Cash Diagram

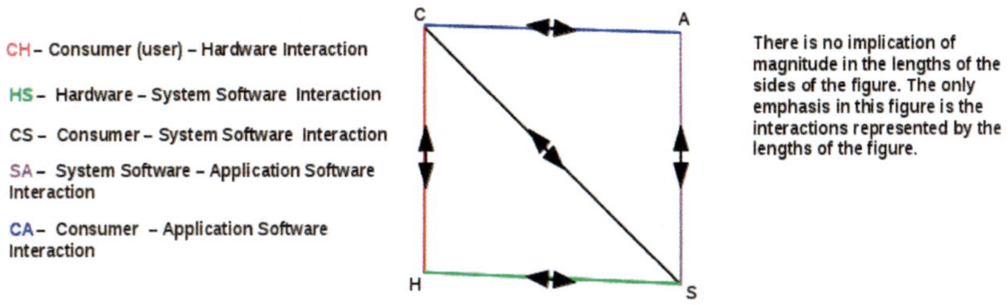

Figure 6.3 – The CASH Diagram

Figure 6.3 is the **Cash Diagram**. It is a conceptual diagram of the interactions in the software's computing space in a stand alone computer. These interactions are:
(1) **Consumer - Hardware Interaction**.
(2**) Hardware - System Software Interaction.**
(3) **Consumer - System Software Interaction.**
(4) **System Software - Application Software Interaction.**
(5) **Consumer - Application Software Interaction.**
All **but (1) are software interactions.**

Consumer-Hardware Interaction
interaction between the user of a computer and the computer itself. An obvious Consumer-Hardware Interaction is the turning on of the power to a computer. The electric signal received by the computer then starts the sequence of interactions inside the computer. The use of input devices such as keyboards, mice, optic devices, fingers, remote controls are other examples of Consumer-Hardware Interactions. The fundamental purpose for this interaction is to have the software inside the hardware perform specific tasks on behalf of the user of the computer.

Hardware-System Software Interaction

Interaction begins once the computer is turned on. The set of System Software called the ***Basic Input/Output System (BIOS)*** which is stored in ROM is responsible for implementing the interaction. The ***BIOS*** consists of the *device drivers* for the hardware units and a program called the ***Boot Loader***. The device drivers are responsible for running diagnostics checks to make sure the hardware units are functioning properly. This process is called ***Power-On-Self-Test (POST)***. ***Post Codes*** (which are two digit symbols) and ***Beep Code*** (which is the sound of a beep) are used to communicate the result of the diagnostic checks of the hardware units. The Boot Loader is responsible for loading the operating system from the hard disk into memory. This process is called ***Booting***. The operating system has to be available to the boot loader if the booting process is to be successful. So, the operating system has to be installed if it is not already on the hard disk or on some secondary storage device. The installation process usually involves getting the operating system from its vendor and running the set-up program of the operating system. During booting, the boot loader reads the ***Master Boot Record*** (MBR) which is the first sector of the hard disk and then copies the code in the MBR to DRAM beginning at location 0X00007C00 (the 0x prefix indicates that the number is hexadecimal). Then it jumps to the address (0x00007c00) so that the code in this address is executed. The objective of the code in the MBR is to load part of the Operating system into DRAM. After part of the operating system is in DRAM, the boot loader hands over control to the operating system so that it can finish loading itself. **A *Dual-Boot*** is the case where there are two operating systems in the computer and a user has to select the preferred operating system during booting. A ***Warm Boot*** is the booting of the computer when the power is on. This is usually accomplished by pressing three keyboard keys. In many computers, a warm boot is accomplished by simultaneously pressing the control key (CTRL), ALT and DEL keys of the keyboard.

A ***Cold Boot*** is the booting of the computer by turning on the power to the computer. The interactions of utility programs such as the back-up, disk partition and disk defragmenter utilities with hardware are other examples of Hardware-System Software Interactions.

Consumer-System Software Interaction

Interaction begins after the operating system loads itself into memory, it presents itself to the user as a *user interface*. This *user interface* can either be a text-based user interface or a graphical user interface (GUI). The operating system is then ready to receive orders as to what task the user wants it to initiate. The order is usually to load an application software or other system software that are used to maintain or repair hardware.

System Software-Application Software Interaction

Interaction is at the heart of Application Software functions. The Application Software requires the services of the System Software, especially the Operating System, often. Some examples of *System Software-Application Software Interaction* are**:**

(1) ***Application Software Installation***: a new application software is usually installed in a computer by the operating system before it is available for use.

(2) ***Loading Application Software***: The Loading of an application software is the copying of the application software from a storage device to the main memory (RAM) of the computer that will run it. The operating system is responsible for loading application software. The loading process requires a System Software-Application Software Interaction.

(3) ***Time Sharing***: is the allocation of execution time by the operating system to several programs or instances of a program in a manner that gives the appearance of simultaneous execution of the programs. The operating system implements time sharing by allocating time slices of very short duration (for example 50 milliseconds) to each of the programs being executed. Suppose programs x, y and z are being executed. The operating system executes x for 50 milliseconds after which x is suspended and y is executed for 50 milliseconds after which y is suspended and z is executed for 50 milliseconds after which z is suspended and execution returns to x. This taking-turns is called Context-switching. It happens so fast that humans perceive the programs as being executed simultaneously but at a reduced speed. The monitoring of the time slices and the suspension of program execution at the end of a time slice is implemented by a timing device which has a timer device driver that is incorporated into the operating system. The timing device initiates a hardware interrupt at the appropriate time. The timer device driver then saves all register values pertaining to the program being executed at the time of the hardware interrupt. The operating system then restores all register values pertaining to the next program in line for execution, especially the value of the Program Counter (PC) of the program. This value allows the CPU to jump from the operating system to the program in line for execution and to the point where it was last suspended. There are many different processes being executed inside the CPU at any given time. These processes are instances of software execution. For example, three users running one application software at the same time corresponds to three processes. The operating system is responsible for interacting with these processes in order to coordinate their activities.

(4) Software Interrupt: is the signal sent to the operating system by the CPU indicating an application software's request to use a hardware unit. The operating system then calls on the device driver of the hardware to implement the system call.

Consumer-Application Software Interaction

Interaction occurs whenever a user uses an application software. The fundamental aspects of the interaction are:
(1) *Interaction Mode*: a *Consumer-Application Software Interaction* occurs in the context of an *interaction mode*. *Text*, *Graphics* (GUI), *Touch-based* and *speech-based* modes are common interaction modes.
(2) *Interaction format*: the *command format* and *file format* are the standard format for *Consumer-Application Software Interaction*. Users send commands and use *files* in their interactions.

6.4 The Dynamic Space of Computer Networks

A Computer Network is multiple computers connected to one another. How the computers are connected is called the network's ***Topology***. The span of the network, that is, its extent is called the ***Area*** of the network. The communication standards of the network is called the ***Protocol*** of the network. A computer in the network is called a ***node*** or ***host***.

6.4.1 Computer Network Topology

A Network's topology is either a ***Physical Topology*** which is the shape formed as a result of the physical layout of the network's computers, or a ***Logical Topology*** which is the map of the *data-path* of the network. The basic types of computer network topologies are: ***bus***, ***ring***, ***star***, ***tree*** and ***mesh***. A combination of any of these five basic topologies can be used to build a complex ***hybrid topology***.

Bus Topology: figure 6.4.1.

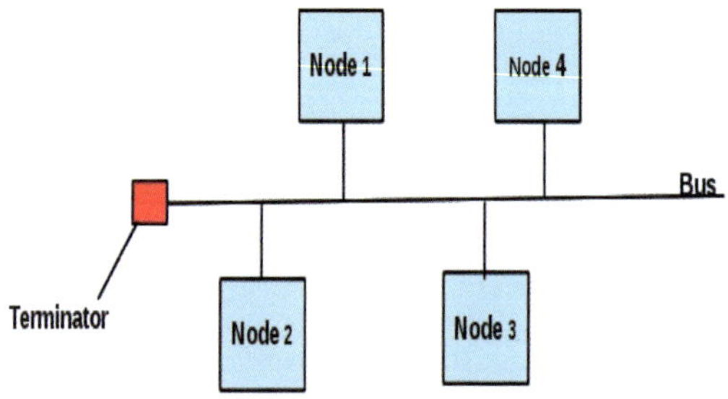

Figure 6.4.1 - Bus Topology

Each *node* is connected to a single main cable called the *bus* or *backbone*. A signal sent to a *node* in the network travels in both directions to all *nodes* connected to the bus cable until it finds the intended recipient. If a *node's* address does not match the intended address for the data, the *node* ignores the data. The *node* accepts the data if its address matches the address of the transmitted data.

The bus topology is simple. However, its principal disadvantage is that a bus failure affects all the *nodes* on the network. The end point of a linear bus is usually terminated with a device called a *terminator* because when the electrical signal reaches the end of the bus, the signal *echoes* back down the line, causing unwanted interference. The terminator prevents this *echo*.

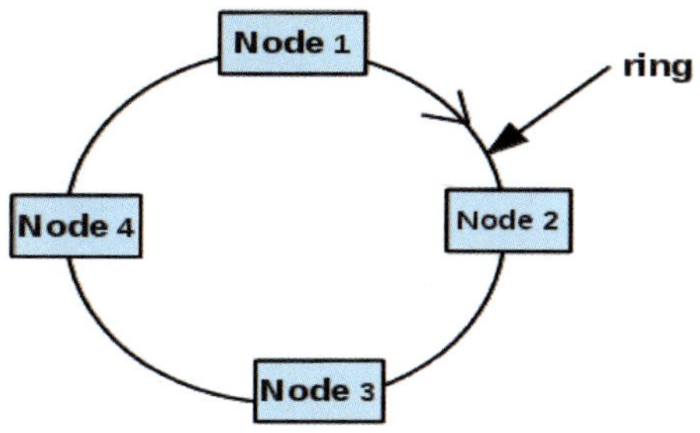

Figure 6.4.2 – Ring Topology

Ring Topology: figure 6.4.2. N*odes* form a ring or a circle. A signal loops through the ring in one direction (anticlockwise or clockwise). The Signal is strengthened as it loops through the ring by each unintended recipient then put back in the ring until the intended recipient accepts it. A failure in any part of the ring affects all the *nodes* connected to the ring.

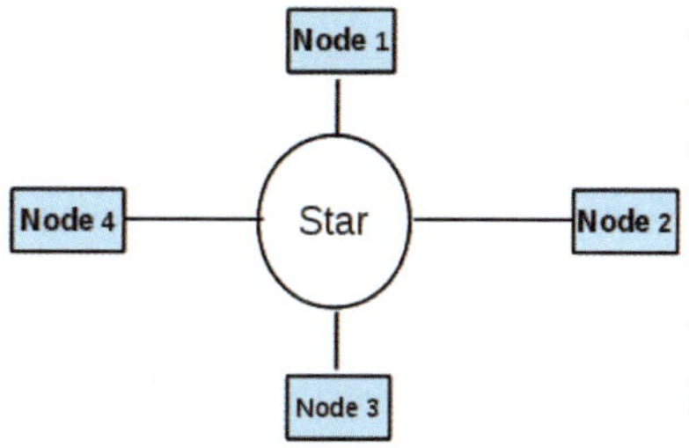

Figure 6.4.3 – Star Topology

Star Topology: figure 6.4.3 *Nodes* are connected to a central device called the *hub*. The *hub* is the entry point for the signal and from the *hub* the signal is sent to the intended host in the network. A hub failure affects all the devices connected to it

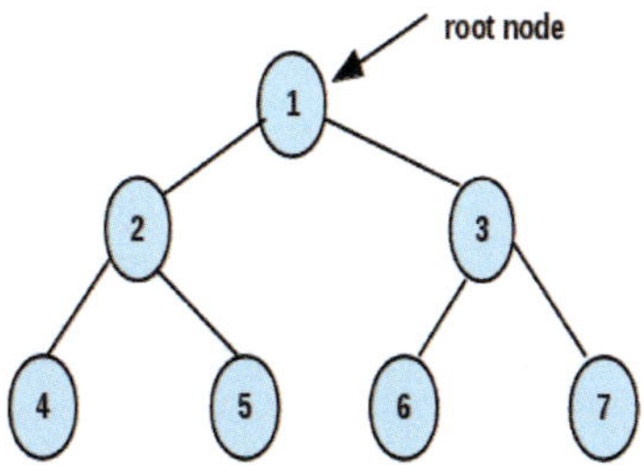

Figure 6.4.4 – Tree Topology

Tree Topology: figure 6.4.4. T A combination of the bus and star topology. Its *nodes* are arranged in ordered levels. The *root node* is the highest level. Point-to-point connection is then used to connect the *root node* to one or more nodes to form the next level beneath it. Levels are formed downward in this manner. There is no restriction on the number of levels that can be formed.

However, too many levels can be complex and difficult to manage. Each node at a given level has a specific number of nodes connected to it from the next lower level in the hierarchy. This number is called the *branching factor (f)* of the tree. The *branching factor* is independent of the total number of nodes in the network. Therefore, ports can be added to nodes without any effect upon the total number of nodes in the network.

Mesh Topology: figure 6.4.5.

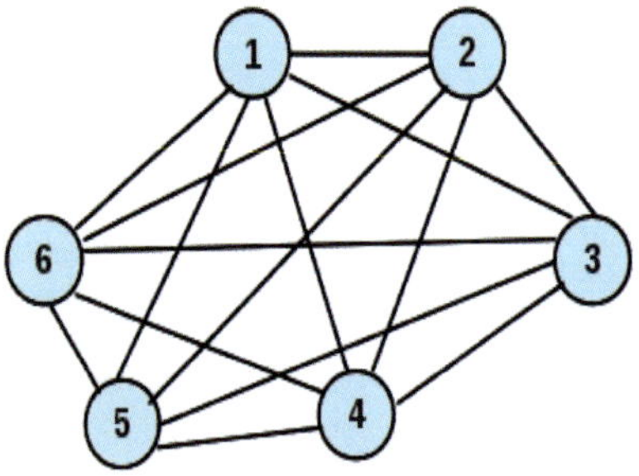

Figure 6.4.5 – Fully Connected Mesh Topology

The mesh topology emphasizes variable data-paths from source to destination. Messages sent on a mesh network can take any of several possible paths from source to destination. The *Internet* is an example of a network that uses mesh routing. A *full mesh network* has every *node* directly connected to every other *node*. A *partial mesh network* has some of its *nodes* indirectly connected to other *nodes*.

6.4..2 Area Networks

The whole idea of computer networking requires that the connected computers be some distance apart. The extent of this distance is called the *Area of the Network*. The idea to connect computers together came out of the communication needs of computer users who wanted to use their computers to communicate with other computer users at different locations. Prior to 1970, computers were primarily used in government agencies, the universities and large corporations. Consequently, the first meaningful computer networks came out of these institutions. The initial communication needs of the computer users in these institutions were local in nature.

So the networks they created covered local areas, that is, within the institutions. Today, computer networks extend far beyond local areas and the concept of Area Network has become an important method by which networks are classified. Some common types of area networks are:

(1) ***Local Area network*** (LAN): a LAN spans a relatively short distance; for example an office building, a school, home, or occasionally a group of buildings that are close together. LANs are usually owned and managed by a single person or organization.

(2) ***Wireless Local Area Network*** (WLAN): a LAN based on WiFi wireless network technology.

(3) ***Wide Area Network*** (WAN): connected LANs located in various geographic areas. It spans a very large distance. Electronic devices called ***routers*** connect LANs to a WAN. The internet is an example of a WAN. A WAN is not owned by a single person or organization. Rather, it is collectively owned by the sub-nets that formed it and managed by a consortium that reflects its ownership.

(4) ***Metropolitan Area Network***: a MAN spans an area greater than that of a LAN but less than that of a WAN. For example, A city-wide network owned by a city government or the network of a large organization.

(5) ***Campus Area Network*** (CAN): also called Cluster Area Network, CAN consists of multiple LANs but it spans an area smaller than that of a MAN. For example, a university-wide network restricted to a campus of the university.

(6) ***System Area Network*** (SAN): this SAN links high-performance computers with high-speed connections in a cluster.

(7) ***Storage Area Network*** (SAN): this SAN connects servers to data storage devices through *Fiber Channel* (a high speed connectivity).

(8) ***Personal Area Network*** (PAN): a subset of a LAN. It is a personal network that spans an area of about 30 feet and consists of personal computational devices such as a laptop, smartphone etc. The devices can then interact through *bluetooth*

(9) ***Body Area Network*** (BAN): also known as ***Wireless Body Area Network*** (WBAN) or a ***Body Sensor Network*** (BSN). It is a wireless network of wearable computing devices placed within, on or in the immediate vicinity of the human body. The network consists of several miniaturized body sensor units (BSUs) together with a single body central unit (BCU).

(10) ***Wireless Body Area Network*** (WBAN) or a ***Body Sensor Network*** (BSN). It is a wireless network of wearable computing devices placed within, on or in the immediate vicinity of the human body. The network consists of several miniaturized body sensor units (BSUs) together with a single body central unit (BCU).

6.4.3 Computer Network Devices

Software interactions on a computer network is made possible by the physical devices that transport, route and enhance signals placed on the network. Some of these devices are:

(a) ***Network Interface Controller*** (NIC): this device is also called the ***Network Interface Card*** and is used to connect a computer to a computer network. A NIC allows computers to communicate over a computer network and has a unique 48-bit serial number called a ***Media Access Control*** (MAC) address, which is stored in ROM. Vendors purchase blocks of addresses from the Institute of Electrical and Electronics Engineers (IEEE) and assign a unique address to each controller at the time of manufacture.

(b) ***Wireless Network Controller*** (WNIC): this device connects a computer to a wireless computer network. A WNIC allows computers attached to it to communicate by LAN.

(c) ***Transport Media***: cables, satellite, etc.

(d) ***Hub***: connects multiple hosts. Signal from a hub goes to all hosts connected to it.

(e) ***Router***: used to route data to the next point on a network as the data travels to its ultimate destination.

(f) ***Repeater***: used to amplify or regenerate data signals on the network as they travel to their destination.
(g) ***Switch***: connects hosts in a network and sends data to its destination on the network.
(h) ***Bridge***: this device is used to connect multiple network segments.
(i) ***Brouter***: a device that acts both as a router and a bridge.
(j) ***Gateway***: this device is used to interface two networks with different protocols.
(k) ***Modem***: this device is used to encode digital signals in an analog signals (modulation) so that the digital signals can be transmitted over an analog network and to decode the analog signals (demodulation) to extract the digital signals in it at the end of the transmission. A modem is used for a computer to computer communication over a telephone network.

6.5 Software Interactions in Computer Networks

Software interactions in a stand-alone computer are basic request-response interactions: an application software requests a service from the system software; the system software responds and implements the service then returns execution to the application software. In the case of a computer network, this basic scenario is expanded to include a transmission component because both the request and the response are implemented some distance away from the point of origin of the request. Consequently, the software interactions in a computer network can be summarized as a basic multiple-layered request-connect-response interactions. The transmission component of this scenario which is indicated by the connect phase is very important because without it the network concept falls apart. In other words, the resources of hosts on a computer network can not be requested or delivered without an efficient delivery method.

The rules that govern software interactions in a computer network are the *network's protocols* and are implemented by the network software called the ***protocol stack*** of the network. Sometimes the term ***protocol suite*** is used in place of protocol stack. Actually, *protocol suite* is the definitions of the protocol while *protocol stack* is the software implementation of the definitions. The *protocol stack* is usually incorporated into the operating system running in the network hosts. It is called a *stack* because of the layering of the software that implements the modularized network tasks. it usually takes several protocols to implement a network interaction. This is because there are several layers of tasks involved and all of the tasks may not require the same rules for interacting with each other. So the stack refers to the layering of the protocols.

A protocol's specifications consist of two conceptual parts:
(1) ***Packet Specification***. The packet specification describes the physical organization of the data to be transmitted over the network. Data to be transmitted is segmented into packets. Each packet contains the bit representation of important information such as the source and destination hosts addresses, other control information

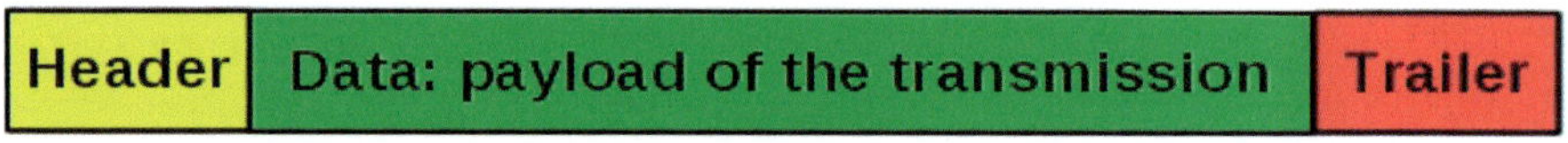

Figure 6.5.0 – Conceptual Packet Specification

and the data itself. Figure 6.5.0 shows the conceptual components of a packet specification: the ***header*** which informs the receiving layer about the characteristics of the data being sent to it; the ***payload*** which contains the data itself and the ***trailer*** which contains error checking information. Each layer sees the *request* sent to it as purely data and adds a header to the request before sending it to the next layer down the stack.

(2) ***Logic Specification***: defines the rules governing interactions between adjacent protocols or interactions between peer-protocols on both the source and destination hosts. Logic specifications are based on state diagrams which indicate the actions to be taken when a given event occurs; for example, authentication, error detection and congestion control actions are based on protocol logic specifications.

The design of protocols can be ***monolithic*** or ***layered.*** A Layered protocol is implemented as a protocol stack: each protocol layer is responsible for a different task. This modularization is flexible with respect to scalability (the addition or deletion of layers as needed), reduces complexity and makes reuse and configuration possible. The monolithic implementation of protocols has no layered protocols. The protocol codes are tightly coupled to create a single seamless network software. Comparatively, the monolithic design uses hardware resources more efficiently than the layered design. However, the inherent non-scalability of monolithic protocols makes them difficult to adapt to a changing programming environment.

Figure 6.5.1 is the **Cash Diagram** in network scenarios. The *Cash Diagram* remains valid in computer network interactions. The only adaptation is that one more basic interaction is added to the former list of five interactions. This sixth interaction is ***hardware – hardware*** interaction.

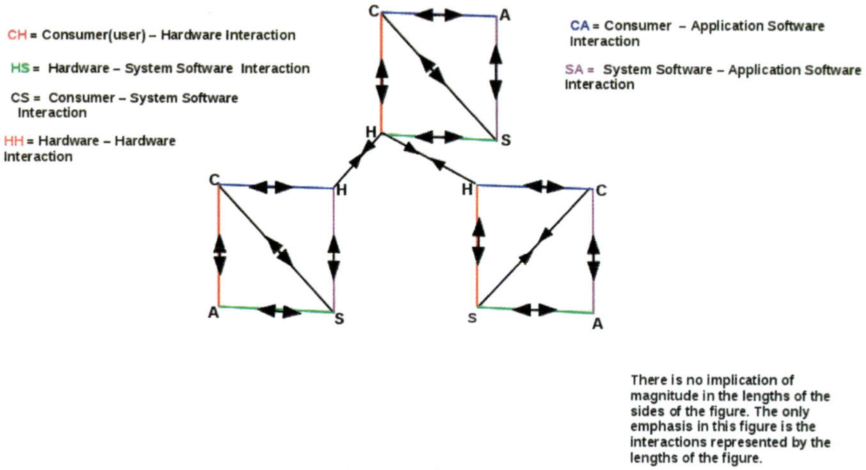

Figure 6.5.1 – The CASH Diagram in Network Scenarios

Networks exist so that the hosts that form the network can interact. The nature of interactions among hosts is dependent on their respective needs and wants as members of the network. The interactions range from the simple sharing of information to the complex buying, selling and social interactions.

Computers on a network are subject to rules and guidelines called ***protocols***. Prior to 1984, there were various types of protocols because of the variability in computer networks components such as topology, area spanned and network devices. In 1984, ***the International Organization for Standardization*** (ISO) decided to establish a standard framework that could be used to address the problems associated with data communication over a network consisting of diverse equipment and applications. This standard is generally known as the ***Open System Interconnections (OSI) Model***.

6.5.1 The Open System Interconnections (OSI) Model

Intuitively, the OSI as established by ISO makes sense. Suppose *computer A* and computer *B* are hosts on a computer network and *B* is willing to share some of its resources with *A*. It is appropriate that B requires that A's request meet the following guidelines: identity of the application software making the request must be known; request must be properly packaged when presented; *A* must notified *B* before the request is sent; request must be properly transported through the pathway that connects A and B. These guidelines and several others are implicit in the OSI model.

The OSI Model consists of seven layers (figure 6.5.2): The layers can be examined from top to bottom (7 - 1) or from bottom to top (1 – 7). Figure 6.5.2 shows the layers beginning with the top layer (the 7th layer):

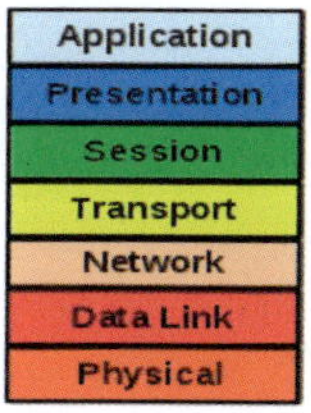

Figure 6.5.2 – The 7 Layers of the OSI Model

(7) ***Application Layer***: is the top-most layer of the seven layered of the (OSI) network model. This layer provides the interface for users and application processes to access network services. Traffic data is often generated in this layer. The Hyper Text Transfer Protocol (HTTP) used by a web browser to retrieve a web page from a web server; the Simple Mail Transfer Protocol (SMTP) used to send emails and the File Transfer Protocol (FTP) used to transfer files from one computer to another are examples of the protocols in this layer. The Application Layer is not referring to the Application Software in the hosts computers, rather it is an interface for the application software; for example, the web browser is an application software that a network user uses to request web pages but the HTTP protocol is an Application Layer protocol that the web browser needs to implement the request of the web pages.

(6) ***Presentation Layer***: this layer translates data contained in the request made by the Application Layer into network format. It is responsible for the syntax and semantics of the information transmitted. Data compression and encryption is also carried out in this layer. The ASCII, EBCDIC, MIDI, MPEG and JPEG protocols are examples of protocols in this layer.

(5) ***Session Layer***: this layer controls the communication link (called a session) between the source and destination hosts. It is responsible for initializing, maintaining and closing the communication link. It controls the right to transmit data. In practice, the Session Layer is often combined with the Transport Layer. The SQL and RPC protocols are examples of protocols in this layer.

(4) ***Transport Layer***: this layer is responsible for packaging the data to be sent to the destination host into smaller bytes bundles called ***packets***. Simultaneous multiple requests from source host are multiplexed at this layer before they are sent to the bottom layers. This layer is responsible for identifying the logical order of these packets and their transport to the destination host. The destination host sends acknowledgments (ACKs) when it receives the packets. In the event that packets are lost during transmission, this layer re-transmits the packets.

The Transport Layer at the destination host is responsible for opening transmitted packets and reconstructing the original data from them. It de-multiplexes the multiplexed data it receives from the bottom layers and determines the appropriate application for the requests. Port numbers are used to enable multiplexing and de-multiplexing. Port numbers identify the originating network application on the source host and destination network application on the destination host. TCP (Transmission Control Protocol) and UDP (User Datagram Protocol) are the protocols operating at the Transport Layer. UDP is not a connected transmission and does not have the acknowledgment features of TCP. So it is indifferent to data loss during data transmission.

(3) ***Network Layer***: this layer addresses packets, determines the best path or route to their destination, and manages network problems such as data congestion. The network Layer is also responsible for converting the network addresses to the MAC addresses of the machines. Conflicts resulting from different addressing schemes of different networks are resolved at the Network Layer. Routers work at this level by sending the packets along the network. Routers direct the data packet generated by Network Layer using information stored in their routing tables. The routing table is a list of available destinations that are stored in the router's memory. The Internet Protocol (IP) operates in this layer. Other protocols in this layer are: ICMP, ARP, PING.

(2) ***Data Link Layer***: this layer encloses traffic data sent into a frame with address information and error checking capabilities. Cyclic Redundancy Check (CRC - a set of trailing data bytes in a message used to determine if an error occurred in a message) is used for the error detection at this level. If at the receiving end the CRC fails at this level there is a request back to the sender for re-transmission of this packet. The Data Link Layer is logically divided into two sub-layers: the ***Media Access Control*** (MAC) Sub-layer which determines the physical addressing of the hosts and the ***Logical Link Control*** (LLC) Sub-layer which is responsible for synchronizing frames, error checking, and flow control. Some specific functions of the data link layer are:

(a) It establishes and terminates the logical link between two nodes.

(b) It controls frame transmission. When no frame buffers are unavailable, it informs the transmitting node to halt transmission.

(c) It acknowledges successfully transmitted data and re-transmits when necessary.

(d) It creates frame boundaries.

(e) It checks for frame integrity.

(f) It controls access to and use of the physical medium.

The IEEE 802.222, 802.323, 802.524 protocols operate in the Data Link layer.

(1) ***Physical Layer***: this layer establishes the physical point to point connection between computers. It maintains and ends the connection. This layer is responsible for the actual interpretation of the bit stream into the electrical signals transmitted through physical media such as the Network Interface Card (NIC) and cables. Some specific functions of the physical layer are:

(a) It maps signal state to a binary 1.

(b) It determines how the receiving host knows when a "bit-time" starts.

(c) It determines how the receiving host delimits the frame.

(d) It determines transmission technique: whether bits will be transmitted by base band (digital) or broadband (analog) signaling.

The Physical Layer is limited to the processes needed to place the communication signals over the media, and to receive signals coming from that media. The transmission media are not part of the Physical Layer. They are referred to as Layer 0 of the Open Systems Interconnection (OSI) Model. The IEEE 802.323, 802.524 protocols operate in this layer.

6.5.2 Network Implementation of The OSI Model

All the interactions of the ***Cash Diagram*** in a network scenario are implicit in the OSI Model. The interactions starts with the *Customer-Application Software Interaction* when a user on a *source hos*t on the network calls up an Application Software that initializes the user's *request*. The *software implementation part* (layers 7 through 4) of the OSI Model is constituted by *Application Software-System Software Interactions*. The ***s****oftware and hardware implementation part* (layers 3 through 1) of the OSI Model is constituted by *System Software-Hardware Interactions*. The electrical signals that represent the initial request are transmitted via the *Hardware-Hardware Interactions*. This layer is referred to as ***Layer 0* of the OSI Model.**

The following key aspects of the OSI model make it a useful template for implementing network protocol stack:
(1) ***Layering***: the delegation of tasks to distinct protocol layers improves efficiency, scalability and adaptability.
(2) ***Data Encapsulation and De-Encapsulation***: each layer validates the data submitted to it with its stamp of receipt. In other words, on receipt of data, the receiving layer adds its header (sometimes a layer also includes a trailer) to the data received before passing it on to the next layer. The data is de-encapsulated in the receiving host.

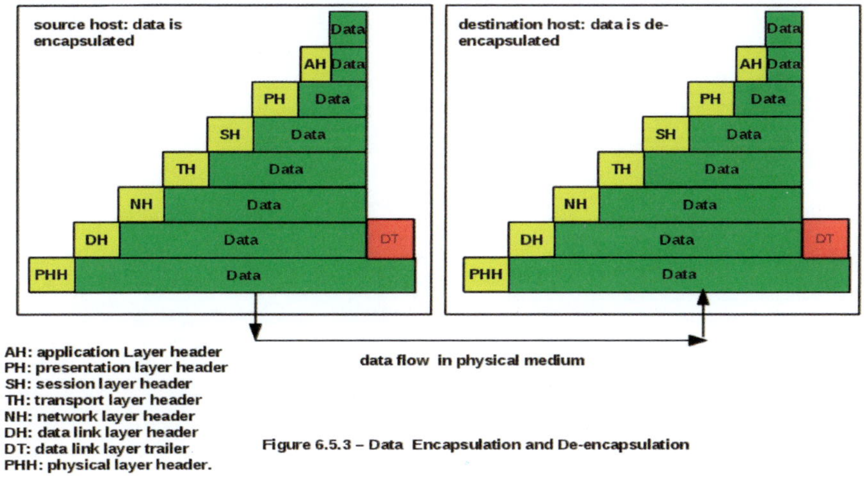

Figure 6.5.3 – Data Encapsulation and De-encapsulation

Figure 6.5.3 illustrates data encapsulation and de-encapsulation in OSI Layers. Encapsulation is carried-out at the source host. Each successive layer adds its header to inform the next layer about the data being submitted to it. From the perspective of each layer, everything other than its header is data. At the application, presentation and session layers, the request is identified as a ***Protocol Data Unit*** (PDU). At the transport layer the *PDU* is identified as a ***Segment***. At the network layer, the ***segment*** is identified as a ***Packet***. At the data link layer, the ***packet*** is identified as a ***Frame*** and a ***trailer*** is attached to it before it is submitted to the physical layer where the *frame* is identified as ***Bits***.

When the *bits* coded as *electric signals* arrive at the *destination host*, *de-encapsulation* which is the reverse of encapsulation is carried-out until the application layer of the destination host receives the request from the source host.
(3) ***Triadic Layer Interactions***: each layer in the source host (excluding the application and physical layers) interacts with its adjacent layers and its peer in the destination host.

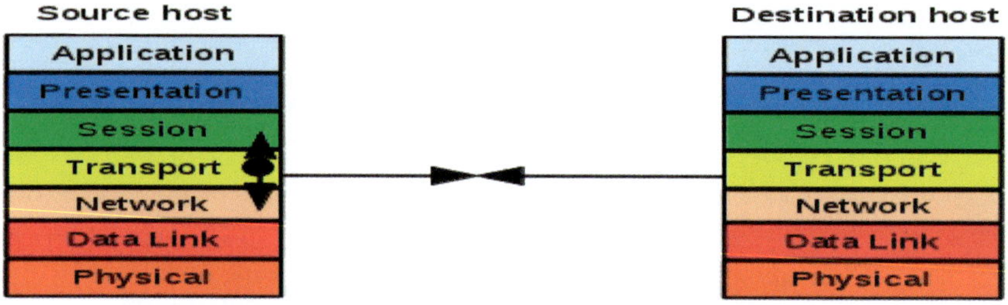

Figure 6.5.4 – The transport layer interactions with the session layer, the network layer and its peer in the destination host

Figure 6.5.4 illustrates the triadic interactions of the transport layer of the source host with the session layer which is above it, the network layer which is below it and its peer, the transport layer in the destination host. These triadic interactions make data encapsulation and de-encapsulation possible. It is also through these triadic interactions that the downward flow of data through the protocol layers of the source host and upward flow through the protocol layers in the destination host, is implemented.

6.5.3 The (TCP/IP)

The use of the OSI model is not mandatory. Consequently, there are several other network protocols in use. Some of the more popular network protocols are: the Transfer Control Protocol/Internet Protocol (***TCP/IP***) model, the ***Microsoft Networking Protocol*** and ***Appletalk***. This section briefly describes the TCP/IP model because of its historical and current importance in computer networking.

The ***TCP/IP*** model is sometimes called the ***DoD*** model because it was initially commissioned by the Defense Advance Research Projects Agency (DARPA) of the United States Department of Defense. It is also called the ***TCP/IP 4 layer protocol*** because it consists of four layers (***application***, ***transport***, ***network*** and ***link***); or the ***Internet Protocol*** because of its prevalent use in the internet. The four layers of the TCP/IP model are:

(1) ***Application Layer***: this layer provides both the user interface for the use of network services and formats the data for the transport layer.

(2) ***Transport Layer***: this layer is responsible for establishing the ports connection for process to process communication between source host and destination host. It controls the flow of data transmission and ensures reliable transmission of data.

(3) ***Network Layer***: this layer handles network and routing functions. It is responsible for ensuring that the transmitted data reach their destination and reporting transmission errors.

(4) ***Link Layer***: this layer describes the local network topology, its networking methods and the interface needed to communicate with hosts in a neighboring network.

6.5.4 The Internet - A Wide Area Network (WAN)

The Wide Area Network is by far the most complex area network. It is in essence a composite of Local Area Networks (LANs). The Internet is currently the most expansive Wide Area Network. The fact that a WAN is a composite of LANs raises some key questions: How are LANs connected to form a WAN? Who owns a WAN? How does data move through a WAN?

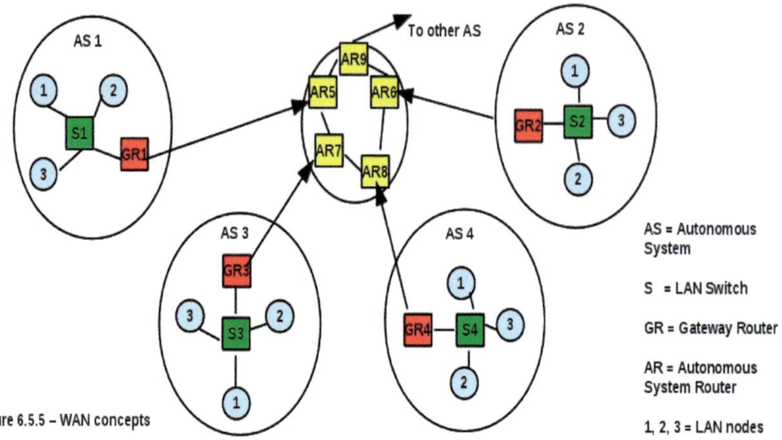

Figure 6.5.5 – WAN concepts

WANs Formation: figure 6.5.5 conceptually illustrates a WAN. The building blocks are area networks called ***Autonomous Systems***. An *Autonomous System* is a single network or a group of networks controlled by a single administrative authority. LANs of university campuses and corporations are examples Autonomous Systems. There are four Autonomous Systems in figure 6.5.5 (AS1, AS2, AS3 and AS4). Each AS is represented by a unique numeric ID known as its ***AS number*** and has several nodes connected to a ***switch*** which is connected to an ***Internal Gateway Router*** that is connected to an External Autonomous System Router which is one of the External Autonomous System Routers that form a communication sub-system. These External Autonomous System Routers are responsible for inter-network routing of network data.

The protocol used by the Internal Gateway Router is called the ***Internal Gateway Protocol*** (IGP). The protocol used by the External Autonomous System Routers is called the ***Boundary Gateway Protocol*** (BGP) which in the future may be changed to the ***Inter-Domain Routing Protocol*** (IDRP).

WAN's Ownership: theoretically, a WAN has no single ownership. Instead a consortium that is representative of the owners of the Autonomous Systems that constitute a WAN jointly administer it. However, when the WAN is a very successful one like the Internet, theoretical ownership gets complicated. Let us use the Internet as the example for the discussion of WAN Ownership.

The Internet is the global network space that evolved from the ***ARPANet*** and the ***NSFNet***. The ARPANet was the result of a research project commissioned by the Advance Research Projects Agency (ARPA) of the United States Department of Defense. Three of ARPANet key contributions to the Internet are: ***packet switching***, ***TCP/IP Protocol*** and ***Backbone***. We shall revisit these terms later. The NFSNet is the collection of networks established by the National Science Foundation. The NFSNet program facilitated the commercialization and spread of the network space that evolved into the Internet and influenced the selection of the networks that are today part of the internet backbone.

So why can't the United States own the internet? After all they started it. Although The United States poineered the organization of the networks that evolved into the internet and the technologies that drive it, the internet has gone well beyond its borders and millions of the resources that make the internet a successful WAN are owned by other entities. Herein lies the complexity of the ownership issue. The debate goes on. Currently, the internet is primarily under the administration of the ***Internet Corporation of Assigned Names and Numbers*** (ICANN).

ICANN controls the assignment of IP addresses through the ***Internet Assigned Numbers Authority (IANA)***. ICANN allocates IP addresses to five ***Regional Internet Registries (RIR)*** which then allocates them to ***Internet Service Providers (ISP)*** and other organizations. The RIR are:

(1) ***African Network Information Centre (AfriNIC)*** for Africa
(2) ***American Registry for Internet Numbers (ARIN)*** for the United States, **Canada,** several parts of the **Caribbean** region, and **Antarctica.**
(3) ***Asia-Pacific Network Information Centre (APNIC)*** for Asia, Australia, New Zealand, and neighboring countries
(4) ***Latin America-Caribbean Network Information Centre (LACNIC)*** for Latin America and parts of the Caribbean region
(5) ***Réseaux IP Européens Network Coordination Centre (RIPE NCC)*** for Europe, Russia, the Middle East, and Central Asia.

Clearly the United States controls the Internet even though it may not publicly claim to be the owner. It exerts this control through the Internet Infrastructure which consists of the *Domain Name System*, IP addresses, the TCP/IP protocols, the backbone (routes between ISPs) and the *local loop* (user phone line between user and ISP).

6.5.5 The Domain Name System (DNS)– Apparatus of Control

The *internet* is a network of several million sub-networks and each of these sub-networks has a unique IP address. There are currently two versions of IP addresses: ***IPv4*** and ***IPv6***. IPv4 was until recently the only type of IP addresses. It is a 32-bit number expressed as four groups of 8-bit numbers separated by dots; for example, 182.243.123.12 (IP numbers in decimals are easier to read). Now those responsible for internet policies have calculated that IP addresses generated by the 32-bit numbering scheme will run out soon. Hence IPv6 which is based on a 128-bit numbering scheme. The **Domain Name System (DNS)** assigns unique names to IP addresses and allows internet users to use names in place of the numbers of IP addresses; for example, the name tectechnics.com is much easier to remember than its associated IP number.

This mapping of domain names to IP addresses is very important because it simplifies and facilitates users interactions with the internet and it is one of the reasons for the phenomenal growth of the internet. However, ultimately it is the IP numbers that the computers in the internet recognize and interpret. Essentially, the DNS is an interface between humans and the computers. The replacing of domain names with their assigned IP addresses by the DNS is called *Domain Name Resolution*.

The Domain Name System has a hierarchical tree structure with the *root file* at the top. The United States controls this root file. It is physically located in the United States and ICANN and Verisign, the company in charge of the A-Root-Server. containing the root file have operational contracts with the US. The next level below the root is called the ***Top-Level-Domain*** (TLD) and it is indicated by the last part of the domain name; for example the ".com" in www.tectechnics.com. There are about 20 generic TLDs (e.g. .com, .org, .edu, .net, etc), three US TLDs (.us, .gov, .mil) and about 252 country-code TLDs (e.g. .uk, .ca, .fr, .ng, .de, .ru, .za, .au, etc). The next level below TLD is called the ***Second Level Domain*** (SLD) and is indicated by the second-to-last part of a domain name; for example, the tectechnics in www.tectechnics.com. The two controlling components of the DNS are the root file and the name servers. The root file, also called the **DOT** controls the authoritative information about TLDs. The root file contains the lists of all TLDs and, for each TLD, the name server (a name server stores domain names and their IP addresses), which stores a list of the second-level domain names of the TLD along with their corresponding IP addresses. So by referring to a particular name server, the root file gives that name server control over the domain names in that TLD.

Consequently, all domain names depend on the root file: domain name searches are based on its name servers referral and these name servers assign domain names under the TLDs by the authority of the root file. The implication of this control mechanism is that the root file controls all traffic on the internet and determines whether or not to include a domain name in the Domain Name System.

The United States' control over the allocation of IP address and the TCP/IP protocol is subtle: ICANN the corporation in charge of allocating IP addresses is contractually obligated to the US so it can be influenced. The US government by virtue of its federal power can legislatively change the transport protocol standard from TCP/IP protocol (highly unlikely since it invented the protocol) to some other protocols. Such a legislative change can only occur in the US. However, because of its influence what happens in the US matters.

The United States' control over the *backbone* and the *local loop* is restricted to its territory. Other countries have control over their own *backbone* and *local loop*. However, the United States can exert influence over these backbones through ICANN's policies on regional inter-connectivity.

There is no doubt that the United States has a controlling power over the internet. In the final analysis, the ***right to control*** is what ownership is all about. However, the power the United States has over the internet does not prevent the internet from being vulnerable to disruptions: very smart people with the necessary technical knowledge can seriously disrupt the internet space as we have seen ***hackers*** do many times**.**

6.5.6 Internet Routing

Ultimately, a computer network is as good as its delivery system. A computer network that can not deliver its packets to their intended destinations most of the time, is an unreliable and unsuccessful network. The internet is successful because of its efficient delivery system and as we have seen, the network protocol stack is a primary component of its delivery system. The other components of the delivery system are the devices such as the routers that move the packets along and the Autonomous System infrastructure of the internet. In this section we examine how these components work together to effect a successful delivery system.

The internet is made up of millions of hosts distributed among tens of thousands of networks called Autonomous Systems (AS), each with its unique ID number called the AS number. Consequently, we can classify internet routing into two categories: ***Intra-AS Routing*** which is routing within an AS and ***Inter-AS Routing*** which is routing between ASs. ***Gateway Routers*** connect an AS with other ASs.

(1) ***Intra-AS Routing***: is implemented with an ***Intra-AS routing protoco***l; for example, the ***Open Shortest Path First (OSPF)*** protocol. This protocol determines Intra-router routing, Internal router to Gateway router routing and Gateway router to Gateway router routing.
(2) ***Inter-AS Routing***: is implemented with the inter-AS routing protocol called ***Border Gateway Protocol (BGP)***. BGP functions are::
(a) Propagation of Autonomous Systems IP address ***Prefixes*** among themselves. An Autonomous Systems IP address prefix represents the range of IP addresses associated with a given Autonomous System; for example, the IP address prefix 184.179.0.0/16 represents a range of 2^{16} IP addresses belonging to a specific Autonomous System with a specific AS number.

The Regional Internet Registries allocate IP address Prefixes to organizations. Thereafter, the organizations own the addresses.
(b) Transmission of reachability information to all internal routers within an AS.
(c) Determination of good routes to all outside sub-nets based on reachability information and AS policies which are usually based on the connectivity relationships between ASs.

The BGP implements its functions through a ***BGP Session*** (a semi-permanent connection between routers) established over TCP. Two routers engaged in a BGP Session are called ***BGP Peers***. If the session is between external Autonomous Systems, it is called ***BGP External Session*** (EBGP). A session within an Autonomous System is called ***BGP Internal Session***. BGP internal session is different from intra-AS routing because it carries inter-AS information and they use different protocols. The protocol Open Shortest Path First (OSPF) is an example of intra-AS routing protocol.

BGP advertises routes to Autonomous Systems by propagating routing messages which are based on its comprehensive lists of inter-AS paths. An AS may or may not forward an advertisement for a foreign network because a decision to do so implies that it is willing to carry traffic for that network. Route selection and announcement in BGP are determined by networks' routing policies. These policies are influenced by the business relationship between two connected ASs. Autonomous System relationships can be generally classified as *customer-provider* or *peer-peer*. In a customer-provider relationship, the AS that is the customer pays the AS that is the provider for access service to the rest of the Internet. In a peer-peer relationship the two peer ASs exchange traffic between their respective customers without monetary cost.

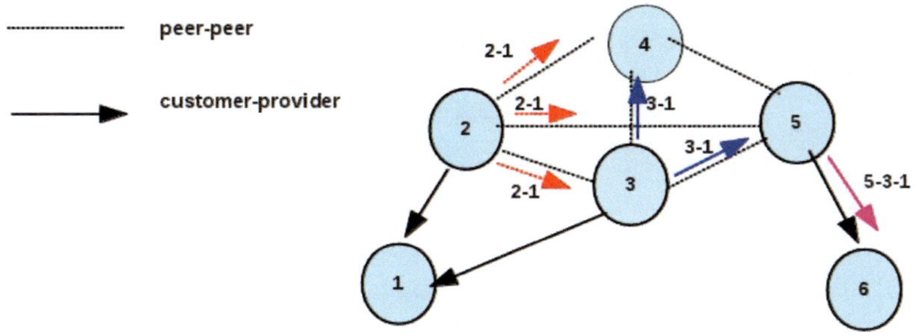

Figure 6.5.6 – AS route propagation

Figure 6.5.6 is a simplistic illustration of how the relationships between neighboring ASs affect routing. In figure 6.5.6, there are six Autonomous Systems (1, 2, 3, 4, 5, and 6). ASs 2, 3 , 4 and 5 have *peer-peer* relationships. AS 1 has a *customer-provider* relationship with ASs 2 and 3 while AS 6 has a *customer-provider* relationship with AS 5. Now, AS 2 announces the *2-1* route to all its peers (3, 4 and 5). AS 3 announces the *3-1* route to only two of its peers (4 and 5). AS 5 announces the *5-3-1* route to its customer (6). In essence, AS 2 is saying to ASs 3, 4 and 5 that '*a route to AS 1 is through me*'. AS 3 is telling only ASs 4 and 5 that '*a route to AS 1 is through me*'. AS 5 is telling only AS 6 that it can get to AS 1 through ASs 5 and 3. Usually, a customer AS does not forward traffic between its providers, nor does a peer AS forward traffic between two other peers. In general Autonomous Systems choose what routes they *import* or *export* to their neighbors based on their respective routing policies. Essentially, when ASs choose their best path, they usually follow the order of customer routes, peer routes, and provider routes. Other criteria used in routing decisions include *shortest AS-PATH* and *NEXT-HOP router*, particularly when an AS has to pick from multiple routes that equally meet the *policy preference criterion*.

Most of the routings on the internet are carried out by Autonomous Systems called *Internet Service Providers (ISPs)*. An ISP's business is to provide *packet* forwarding services between other networks. Hence they are called *transit networks*. ISPs are less that 30% of all the networks that constitute the *internet*. The majority of the networks that make-up the *internet* are called *stub networks* and they do not forward *packets* for other networks. ISPs are at the top of a global routing hierarchy and are used by *stub* networks to access parts of the *internet* that otherwise are unreachable.

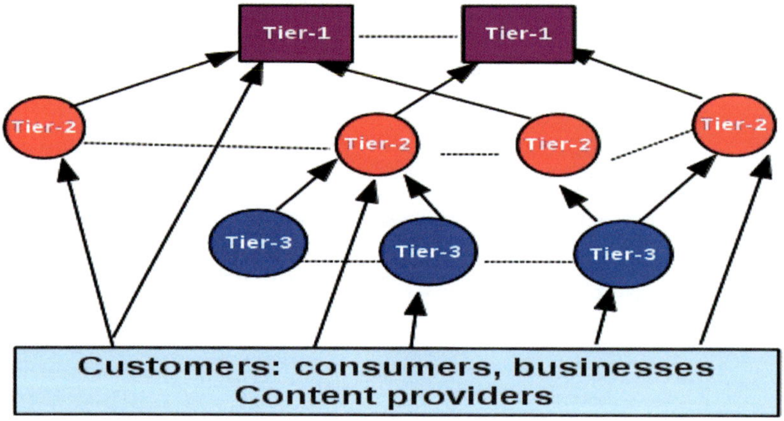

Figure 6.5.7– ISPs Hierarchy

Figure 6.5.7 is an illustration of ISPs hierarchy. Tier-1 ISPs which connect to each other in a fully connected mesh topology are at the top of ISPs hierarchy. Tier-1 ISPs form the core of the global routing infrastructure. The ISPs hierarchical structure is an informal one, that is, the structure is not instituted by any official agency. An ISP tier is based on several criteria some of which include technical capacity and the extent of internet reach or coverage; for example, a tier-1 ISP must have domestic, regional and global coverage and the technical capacity to efficiently implement the connectivities required for such coverage.

Associations between ISPs is either a peer-peer relationship or a customer-provider relationship. Figure 6.5.7 also shows that an ISP can be multi-homed, that is, it can have more than one provider. A peer-peer relationship is usually based on both economic and privacy issues. Strategic peerings can reduce the operational costs of an ISP since such peerings are usually free. On the other hand, over-peering can reduce the customer base of an ISP. Peerings are either private or public. Private peerings are implemented through dedicated connections between peers. Public peerings are implemented through *Internet Exchange Points* (IXPS) which are physical infrastructures maintained by third parties. The IXPs enable the physical connectivities between its ISP members who have the right to choose the members with whom to establish BGP sessions.

6.6 Chapter Summary

There are two general groups of software: application software and system software. Application software are programs that users use to accomplish specific tasks; for example a word processor. System software are programs that interact with hardware on behalf of application software. System software consist of operating systems, utility programs and device drivers. Sometimes all three components of the system software are together called the operating system.

Computer networks are grouped according to the area they span. Local Area Networks (LANS) and Wide Area Networks (WAN) are two important type of networks. WANS are made up of LANS called Autonomous Systems.

Software interactions occur in both a stand-alone computer and in a computer network. All interactions in any software's computing space are indicated in the *CASH Diagram*. They are:
(1) Consumer – Hardware Interaction

(2) Consumer-System Software Interaction
(3) System Software-Application Software Interactions
(4) Consumer-Application software Interactions
(5) System Software-Hardware Interaction
(6) Hardware-Hardware Interaction.

The delivery of a *request* from a source host to a destination host in a computer network is made possible by both network devices such as routers, bridges, gateways and cables; and network software such as the Transmission Control Protocol/Internet Protocol. Network software are modularized into layers that are together called a protocol stack. The International Standard Organization (ISO) established the Open Systems Interconnections (OSI) as a protocol stack standard. However, the use of OSI is not mandatory.

The OSI Model consists of the following seven layers:
(1) The Application Layer
(2) The Presentation Layer
(3) The Session Layer
(4) The Transport Layer
(5) The Network Layer
(6) The Data Link Layer
(7) The Physical Layer

The object of the inter-layer interactions is the Protocol Data Unit (PDU). The PDU moves downward in the source computer from the application layer to the physical layer and as it moves from layer to layer, its data is encapsulated by the respective headers of the layers. It is called a *segment* at the session and transport layers; a *packet* at the network layer; a *frame* at the data link layer and *bits* at the physical layer. At the destination computer, the PDU moves upward from the physical later to the application layer and as it moves from layer to layer it is de-encapsulated. At the application layer, the data sent by the source computer is made available to the appropriate application software in the destination computer

The Internet is a successful WAN. It is a collection of Autonomous Systems about 30% of which are Internet Service Providers. The others are non Internet Service Providers sub-nets. The TCP/IP which is a four-layered protocol suite is the primary mode of transmitting packetized requests from source host to destination host on the internet. The four layers of TCP/IP are: *Application layer*, *Transport Layer*, *Network Layer* and *Link Layer*. The Domain Name System (DNS) is responsible for translating a domain name to its equivalent numeric 32 bits IP address.

7 Software Equilibrium

7.0 What Is Equilibrium

Equilibrium is stability. The notion of equilibrium or stability is usually relative to a reference state within the context of a body of knowledge. Hence there are many types of equilibrium. However, two reference states are commonly used: static state and dynamic state. In other words, there are two possible types of equilibrium within the context of a body of knowledge: ***Static Equilibrium*** which is a stable state without external motion and ***Dynamic Equilibrium*** which is a stable state with external motion. A parked car within the context of the body of knowledge known as mechanics is in static equilibrium while a car moving with uniform velocity is in dynamic equilibrium because there is no net force acting upon it so as to cause it to accelerate. The distinction between external motion and internal motion is made here because internal motions due to sub-atomic and atomic motions occur in all entities.

7.1 Software Equilibrium

A *software* is in *dynamic equilibrium* if it operates according to its owner's specifications, that is, it solves the problem its owner wants it to solve whenever it is in operation. Otherwise, it is in *dynamic disequilibruim*. A *software* is in *static equilibrium* in storage if whenever it is loaded to run, it maintains its *dynamic equilibrium.*

Software equilibrium is usually approached from thee perspective of *disequilibrium.* In other words, *"prevention is better than cure*. It is like wanting to know how to prevent a fire or a flood before they occur. The *disequilibrium* perspective implies that *software equilibrium* can best be realized through the prevention and cure of *software disequilibrium.* Consequently the focus in this chapter is on the causes of *software disequilibrium* and how to prevent and mitigate them.

7.1.1 Causes of software Equilibrium

The causes of software disequilibrium can be broadly grouped into two classes: ***non-malicious causes*** of *software disequilibrium* and ***malicious*** causes of *software equilibrium*.

(1) ***Non-malicious causes***: design, programming and user errors are some of the important causes of non-malicious causes of software disequilibrium. Design and programming errors occur when the specifications of a software are inappropriately designed and coded; for example, the introduction of erroneous code lines or omission of necessary code lines can cause a software to malfunction during its deployment. A poorly documented software can cause users to inadvertently crash the system. The errors or bugs introduced into a software by these causes of software disequilibrium are usually unintentional and therefore non-malicious.

(2) ***Malicious causes***: some of the most serious software disequilibria are caused by malicious software called ***malware***. There are currently many types of *malware* and hybrids of the fundamental types are constantly being created. So it is not possible to showcase everyone of these malware. However, it is possible to examine some of the basic types of malware and the common characteristics of all malware. The following are some of the basic types of malware.

7.1.2 Computer Viruses

A *computer virus* is a type of *malware*.that accesses a computer without detection. It *infects* legitimate programs, data files, or the boot sector of the hard drive by copying itself in these spaces when it is unknowingly executed with legitimate executable programs in the computer. The virus can carry out any number of harmful activities in the computer: it can steal hard disk space, CPU time and private information. It can corrupt data, log user's keystrokes and display a message of choice on user's screen.

Computer viruses are commonly classified according to the spaces they infect. Some of the groups are:

(a) ***Memory-resident viruses***: a memory-resident virus accesses the operating system and loads itself as part of the operating system when the operating system is executed. Thereafter, it remains in RAM until the computer is shut down. A *memory-resident virus* disrupts the functions of the operating system while in RAM; for example, it can intercept the operating system's move to access a target file for *loading* and then *infect* the target file.
(b) ***Non-resident viruses***: a non-resident virus remains in memory only during its execution. While being executed in memory, it scans the disk for targets, infects them and then exits RAM.
(c) ***Macro viruses***: some application software allow *macros* (programs used to implement repetitive tasks) to be embedded in their documents or emails. A *macro virus* (also called *document virus*) is a virus that is written in a *macro* language and embedded into *macro-enabled* documents. The virus is executed when the document is opened and then proceeds to infect the computer.

(d) ***Boot sector viruses***: a *boot sector virus* specifically targets the boot sector or Master Boot Record (MBR) of its host's hard drive or other secondary storage media such as the flash drive, CD/DVD drive. The infection of the boot sector can then disrupt the booting process.

7.1.3 Computer Worms

A *computer worm* is a *malware* designed to self-replicate and spread over a computer network. Unlike the *computer virus* its execution is not dependent on the execution of an existing program. In other words, it does not need to attach itself to an existing program. A *computer worm* may not specifically target the files in a computer. However, such a *worm* often called ***payload free worm*** almost always causes significant disruption in the network it targets.
For example, by consuming bandwidth and causing traffic congestion in the network. *Worms* with ***payloads*** *(the intended harm)* are designed for targeted harm to the resources in the targeted hosts. Some of the harms are: *Denial of Service* (DoD) attacks; deletion and encrytion of files; and the creation of *botnets* (*zombie* network controlled through *backdoors* by worm designers).

7.1.4 Trojan Horses

A *Trojan horse* is a deceitful *malware* that does not self-replicate. It operates by gaining privileged access to the operating system under the disguise of being a useful and desirable program. Thereafter, it offloads its *payload* which often includes the installation of a *backdoor* that is used to gain unauthorized access to the targeted host. Unlike the *computer virus*, a *Trojan horse* does not attempt to *infect* files in a targeted host. Its primary objective is to establish a *backdoor* as an access-point in the targeted host. The *backdoors* established by *Trojan horses* are frequently used by *hackers* to perpetrate various types of harms on the internet: data theft, spying, remote control of the host, use of host as a proxy, etc.

7.1.5 Spyware

Generally, a *spyware* is a *software spy*: it monitors a targeted host's activities, collects and uses the information gathered about targeted entities (persons, organizations, etc) without their knowledge. *Spyware* is mostly used to track and collect information about the web activities of internet users and to display pop-up ads to internet users. However, it can be designed to be malicious. The fact that a *Trojan horse* is a type of *spyware* attests to the malicious capacity of *spyware*. When designed to be malicious, *spyware* can steal bank or credit card account information; redirect web browsers; degrade system performance and cause system wide crashes; etc.
There are numerous ways (known and uknown) in which very bright people can disrupt the equilibrium of *software*. So an attempt to examine all causes of software disequilibrium is usually not an economically smart move. A more productive move from a cost-benefit perspective is to develop and implement a *risk management* plan for *software disequilibrium*.

7.2 Maintaining Software Equilibrium Through Risk Management

The maintenance of software equilibrium is a ***risk*** management issue. ***Risk*** simply means that a loss may occur if an event occurs. An event is a happening; for example, a building on fire is an event. So if we say fire is risky, we mean something valuable can be lost if a fire occurs; for example the loss of lives and property. ***Risk management*** is concerned with figuring out the various scenarios in which the events of interest can occur; the potential losses associated with the occurrences of the events; the different ways to prevent the events from occurring; the different ways to reduce or replace the losses should the events occur; and the integration of these results into an optimal risk management policy.

In the context of software, the event of interest is software disequilibrium. Usually, a wise approach in risk analysis is to first examine how an event of interest can be prevented. If the event is not preventable, then the probabilities of its occurrence and the losses associated with these probabilities are determined and mitigated.

Let us use a familiar scenario to illustrate this notion of ***risk management*.** Suppose that the *event* of interest is the occurrence of a fire in a building. A *risk manager* will determine that such a *fire* can be caused by an unintended human error or the deliberate action of an arsonist. So he or she will make sure that *Fire Safety Rules* as mandated by the Fire Department are implemented in the building and that residents of the building are educated on how to prevent common human behaviors that can cause unintentional fire; for example, making sure that the stove is not left unattended while cooking in the kitchen. These plans are examples of positive procedures to address the risk due to unintended human error. Preventing an arsonist from setting the building ablaze is a more complicated matter because the identity of the arsonist and his intended period of attack may not be known. Nonetheless, the *risk manager* can ensure that the building's perimeter is secured so that it will be difficult for the arsonist to access the building's premises. The *risk manager* will also understand that these precautions do not absolutely guarantee the non-occurrence of fire in the building. In other words, it is possible that fire can still occur in the building either as a result of unintended human error or the deliberate action of an arsonist despite the preventive measures. So the *risk manager* purchases a *fire insurance policy* so that if the building is set ablaze the insurance policy will *mitigate* the impact of the *loss* due to the fire.

In general, *risk management* consists of two components: ***preventive*** component and ***mitigative*** component. The focus of the remainder of this chapter is on the examination of these components in the context of *software equilibrium*.

7.2.1 Preventive Component Of Software Disequilibrium

Software is created by programmers according to specifications. The design of the specifications and the coding of the specifications are the most important stages in the life cycle of any software. A poorly created software is more likely to contain errors (bugs). These errors can make a software vulnerable to software disequilibrium hence they are also called ***Software Vulnerabilities***. Often these vulnerabilities are unknown to the creators of the software at deployment. They become known when very bright hackers discover and exploit them for their malicious campaign. The period from software deployment to when a vulnerability is internally discovered and removed is known as the ***window of vulnerability***. Vulnerabilities are grouped according to their sources:

Software vulnerabilities: due to insufficient testing, poor source code documentation, lack of audit trail, etc.

Hardware vulnerabilities: due to exposure to humidity, dust, unprotected storage, etc.

Network vulnerabilities: due to unprotected communication lines, insecure network architecture, substandard network devices, etc.

Personnel vulnerabilities: due to incompetent personnel, lack of personnel training, disgruntled personnel, etc

Site vulnerabilities: due to unreliable power source, adverse weather (e.g. hurricane, flooding zones), etc.

Organizational vulnerabilities: due to lack of a comprehensive risk management policy.

It is perhaps not always possible to have zero vulnerability. However, the use of very competent designers and programmers can reduce the number of vulnerabilities inadvertently introduced into a software at deployment. Also, the window of vulnerability can be shortened by practicing periodic software testing, monitoring (by anti-virus programs) and auditing. These precautions will reduce the likelihood of software disequilibrium due to design and programming errors.

Non-software vulnerabilities can be prevented by a comprehensive software disequilibrium prevention plan: proper documentation of software and comprehensive training of personnel will reduce personnel vulnerabilities; encrypting data and the establishment of a *firewall* where incoming requests are subjected to the identification, authentication and authorization process, will reduce network vulnerabilities.

7.2.2 Mitigative Component of Software Disequilibrium

The ubiquity of the internet and the complexities of the software and devices that drive it have elevated the risk associated with software disequilibrium. In other words, almost all computing environments are vulnerable to the harmful attacks of malware. The objective of the mitigative component of software disequilibrium is to reduce the adverse impact caused by software disequilibrium when it occurs.

Software equilibrium is desirable to an entity because the entity wants to maintain the ***confidentiality***, ***integrity*** and ***availability*** of its data. When software disequilibrium occurs, this fundamental desire is disrupted and losses are incurred by the entity. There are various types of losses that can be sustained by entities as a result of software disequilibrium. However, these losses can be broadly categorized as either tangible losses or intangible losses. An example of an intangible loss is the loss of the goodwill of customers. Suppose the credit card numbers of customers of a credit card company are always stolen whenever it experiences software disequilibrium. This company will eventually lose some if not all of its customers' goodwill. It will also lose income if its customers cease to do business with it. This scenario illustrates the case in which an entity sustains both tangible and intangible losses.

Now suppose a substantial amount is electronically stolen from the bank account of a customer. If the bank keeps this *disequilibrium* and theft quiet so that no customer is aware of it, there will be no loss of the goodwill of any customer because they would not be aware of the *disequilibrium*. However, the bank must replace the stolen money as soon as possible. This replacement is certainly a tangible loss.

In general, a *software disequilibrium* will always result in at least one tangible loss (the time lost) and at least one intangible loss (the emotional impact of the disequilibrium) to the owner of the space wherein the disequilibrium occurred.

Software disequilibrium implies that the software is non-operational. So a good mitigation plan must have procedures in place to quickly get the software back into operational mode. If the cause of disequilibrium is due to unintended human errors, the errors are determined and corrected. If the disequilibrium is due to an attack by a malware, then it is likely that the anti-malware tools embedded in the software which were supposed to detect the malware failed to do so. A possible reason for such a failure might be that a new vulnerability has been discovered by the attacker. Another possible reason might be that the attacker is just simply too sophisticated and has created a new and an unrecognizable malware. n both cases, the first objective is to find and remove the malware. Thereafter, the vulnerability can be patched. In the extreme case of total disequilibrium, the software can be redeployed. Quick redeployment is only possible if there is a *Back-Up* copy of the software in its most current equilibrium state. This is the reason why the back-up process is the most important mitigative procedure. Back-up is the process of creating duplicates (by copying) of the most current equilibrium state of software and other computing resources and storing the duplicates securely offfline.

Frequent and up-to-date back-ups is an effective method of restoring software equilibrium. Interestingly, despite all the complexities of the interconnectivity of our modern world, it is a simple procedure called ***Back-Up*** that presents a very effective way to mitigate the most undesirable consequence of software disequilibrium which is the the total loss of the software.

Once the ability of the software to operate efficiently is guaranteed, the mitigation plans for the intangible and tangible losses due the disequilibrium can be implemented by the risk management team; for example, plans for restoring stolen data and recovering loss of operational income can be implemented.

7.3 Chapter Summary

A software that operates according to specifications is in *dynamic equilibrium*. It is in *static equilibrium* in storage if whenever it is loaded to run, it maintains its *dynamic equilibrium*.

Software disequilibrium is caused by both unintended errors and by malicious attacks by programs called *malware*.

The best way to maintain *software equilibrium* is to manage the *risks* associated with *software disequilibrium* through the *preventive* and *mitigative* components of *software disequilibrium*.

Problems – Mind Warm-Ups

Containership

Explain why *software* cannot exist in a problemless space.

Identity

(a) How is *software* different from other algorithms?
(b) Every *software* is made up of two components. What are these components?
(c) Explain the following statement: "*software* can be killed and ressurected".
(d) In the beginning, humans created *software* using the computer's native language. Name this language. What is the alphabet of this language?
(e) What are the fundamental stages of *software* creation?

Force

(a) The computer processor is made up of many complex Integrated Circuits (ICs). Name the primary transistors used in these circuits.

(b) The NAND gate and the NOR gate can be used to build other logic gates. How will you build an AND gate from a NAND gate? An Inverter from a NOR gate?
(c) Contrast *Combinational* circuits and *sequential* circuits.
(d) Describe the Von Neumann Computer Architecture.

Motion

(a) Is the movement of *software* from the hard disk to RAM an *external software motion or an internal software motion?*
(b) What are the three stages of *internal software motion*?
(c) Which of the three stages involves the *Control Unit*?
(d) Which of the three stages involves the *ALU*?
(e) Which of the three stages involve the Instruction Register or Program Counter?

(f) What is the purpose of the *stack*?

Change

Give at least one example of each of the following types of *software change*:
(a) Corrective Software Change.
(b) Adaptive Software Change.
(c) Perfective Software Change
(d) Preventive Software Change.
(e) State the three most important postulates of Lehman's Laws with respect to software maintenance and evolution.

Grouping/Interaction

Software is broadly classified into two groups: *system software* and *application software*.
(a) To which group will you assign *device drivers*?
(b) What is the single most important function of the *operating system*?
(c) Give an example of a utility program and explain its function.
(d) To which interaction described in the CASH DIAGRAM will you assign the interaction that occurs in the *decode phase* of the *fetch-decode-execute cycle*?
(e) Explain the *triadic interactions* that occur in layers 2 through 5 of the OSI Model.
(f) An Autonomous System (AS) is a software. True or False?
(g) A tier 1 Internet Service Provider (ISP) must have global coverage and the capacity to implement it. True or False?
(h) ISP(1) is a peer of ISP(2). ISP(2) accepts a *Packet* from ISP(1) for forwarding to ISP(3). It is more likely that ISP(3) is a client of ISP(2). True or False?

Equilibrium

The CEO of a company is looking to hire a risk manager for his company's computer network. He has been presented with the names of individuals who are finalists in the search. This CEO is not interested in any resume or long inteview. He will hire the candidate with the correct answer to the following directives: (a) "State your risk management plan for the *preventive* component of *software disequilibrium* using only *five words*. This *five-word* statement should include the word *prevent* twice". (b) "Use one word to name an old reliable method for mitigating total *software disequilibruim*".

What will be your answers to (a) and (b) if you were one of the candidates vying for the job?

About The Author

Peter Oye Sagay is a research mathematician. He worked as an actuarial professional in a fortune 200 firm, as a software developer and programmer, as a math mentor and tutor volunteer for many years before his current research engagement. He remains active as a private math mentor and tutor of young adults. Some of his protege have become professionals in their respective areas of academic interests. His research interest is E*xistential Continuums*.

His contribution to global thought include:
- Formulation of the *Theory of Existential Continuums*.
- Mathematical proof of the absoluteness of philosophical *Time*.
- Formulation of the direction of the problem solving arrow.
-Explanation of the notion of *conceptual shift of focus* in relation to the great Isaac Newton's (A.D. 1642-1727) concept of *absolute motion.*
- Explanation of the notion *of transient absolute rest (TAR)* as the interpretation of the great Isaac Newton's concept of *absolute motion.*
- Formulation of the Association Principle, etc.

More about the author at ***www.tectechnics.com***.

Printed in Dunstable, United Kingdom

91223991R00063